Window of Peace Quilt

D1608821

Mary E. Dillon

Cover design and interior layout: Anthony Jacobson
Editor: Stephen Levy
Photographs: Paul Garrison

Library of Congress Catalog Card Number 87-51420

ISBN 0-87069-513-4

10 9 8 7 6 5 4 3

Published by

Wallace-Homestead Book Company
201 King of Prussia Road
Radnor, Pennsylvania 19089

Contents

Preface

After many requests for the pattern for the Window of Peace quilt, I decided it was necessary to put the instructions into a form that would be available to my fellow quilters. What follows includes complete instructions for the quilt as well as ideas for other uses for the designs. Since much of my work is done freehand, and the quilt was designed as I stitched, many hours were devoted to transferring the ideas into usable patterns for others. While thorough instructions are given for the quilt, this book is not an attempt to be a complete quilting manual. A working knowledge of the process of making a quilt, as well as some expertise in the craft, is necessary to make a quilt such as the Window of Peace. I hope that what follows will give quilters inspiration and many hours of happy stitching.

Acknowledgments

I gratefully acknowledge the help and support I received from friends and family during the stitching of the Window of Peace quilt and the subsequent writing of this book. First, to my mother, Inez, an accomplished needlewoman. Since the time I was a small child, she has taught me the skills necessary for such work. Without this teaching, and her continued support and patience, this project would not have become a reality. A thank-you also goes to my father, Bill, and other family members who offered suggestions and encouragement.

Individual thanks must go to some special friends. To Regina Schmucker, a best friend who for many years has always been there when needed; an artist could never wish for a better unofficial PR person. To Diane LeFevre, a very special friend, for her help. She gave very generously of her time in reading the manuscript and offering suggestions from a novice quilter's viewpoint. To Jean Brown, a fellow quilter; I am most appreciative of the time she gave to proofread the manuscript. Her expert opinion was most helpful. To Pat Howard, who graciously gave of her time and typing skills to prepare the first draft of the manuscript, I am very thankful.

Finally, I would like to acknowledge and thank all of my co-workers, neighbors, and friends—quilters and nonquilters—who were willing to offer encouraging words and who gave me many positive strokes. Space will not allow mentioning everybody individually, but I do appreciate all of the support and send a big thank-you to everyone.

The Window of Peace Quilt

The Window of Peace quilt consists of a large center medallion depicting a rainbow and a dove, encircled by a border of roses. This is surrounded by 22 blocks representing a variety of flowers. The designs and the use of colors give the illusion of a stained-glass window.

Seventeen individual patterns are given in the directions. While these individual designs are shown as a group in one quilt, the actual number of uses for the patterns are limited only by your imagination. Pillows, wall quilts, sun catchers, and clothing adornment are just a few ideas for alternative uses of the designs. Three or four blocks in a panel work well for a wall hanging or a table runner.

An assortment of sizes can be found within the designs. This allows for greater freedom when adapting the designs to a variety of uses. By using different combinations of squares and rectangles, you can create a number of interesting effects.

The rectangular tulip block can easily be adapted for place mats. Just add borders to increase the design to a usable size. Attractive hangings for use in windows or on walls can be made either by quilting a group of blocks or by simply appliquéing the designs onto backing fabric and then stretching the fabric over a frame such as stretcher bars. This will make a more attractive back while still allowing the light to shine through the design.

Special Techniques

The techniques used in making Window of Peace were developed by quilters so the stained-glass look could be achieved while using fabric as the medium. There are two common methods used to achieve this effect. The technique used in the quilt, the one that will be discussed in this book, involves appliquéing black bias strips over the seams between other fabrics to achieve the look of leading found in stained-glass work. The other method involves using a type of reverse appliqué to achieve the same effect.

Diagram I.
Positioning the Leading

The following designs were developed to be worked in fabric. Because of this, portions of some of the designs may not be technically correct to use for actual stained-glass work. This is part of the artistic freedom that is used to adapt work from one medium to another: The constraints of one technique differ from those of the other, therefore we're able to make design changes when making the adaptations. As an example, certain shapes, such as long, narrow ones, are more likely to break while cutting glass. While cutting fabric, there is no need to worry about areas of stress or possible breakage.

The position of the leading while working with glass is also important, as it provides for strength in the final window. While strength is not a consideration in fabric, creating correct design makes the same rules important for a quilt. As an example, many lead lines coming together can form an unattractive blob when working with glass. This same effect can happen with fabric and in many cases will distract from the design. Diagram 1 illustrates this point.

It also should be noted that some areas appear visually incorrect while looking at the patterns, but they will "correct" themselves as the design is worked in the fabric. A good example of this is the stems of the flowers. These appear exceptionally wide in proportion to other areas of the patterns. But as the leading is applied, the stems will narrow and become proportionate to the other areas of the design. While visualizing the final product that will be achieved from the patterns, notice also, as is the case in many glass windows, some of the natural shapes have been simplified for the purpose of design.

What follows are directions and patterns to make the quilt shown on the front cover. The directions will take you step by step through the process involved in making the quilt. The text will also guide the individual who decides to make design changes to develop a more individualized project.

It is suggested that you first read the complete text prior to starting any work and then follow along step by step as the work progresses. Remember, patience counts with a work such as this. It is not a process that can be hurried; the hours will be well spent in the finished product.

Supplies

Scissors

One pair for fabric and one pair that is suitable for cutting paper, lightweight cardboard, or acetate.

Needles

For appliqué, basting, quilting.

Size 7–size 12 (betweens) are used for quilting. Size will depend on individual preference. Size 7 is the largest, with the sizes decreasing to size 12.

Pins

Fine, brass silk pins work best.

Thread

Black and white cotton or cotton-covered polyester #50 sewing threads. Do not use 100% polyester thread as it may cut into the fabric. The black will be used for making the bias and for the appliqué. The white will be used to stitch the foundations of the blocks together.

A variety of colors in quilting thread. Again, use 100-percent cotton or cotton-covered polyester thread.

Light-colored thread for basting.

Thimble

Worn on the middle finger of the hand used for quilting. Some quilters also wear one on the hand beneath the quilt. Many types are available.

Experiment and find one that is comfortable.

Beeswax

Ruler

Yardstick

Pencils

For making patterns and marking seams on fabric. Never mark on fabric with an ink pen, and keep ink away from your fabric while you're stitching. Ink may spot the fabric, or it may bleed on the fabric while it is being washed.

Felt-Tip Pen

To be used for making patterns. Do not use near fabrics.

Right-Angle Triangle or an L-Angle

To make squares.

Masking Tape

One-quarter-inch wide.

Tracing Paper

Quilt Frame or Quilt Hoops

Sheet of Acetate or Thin Cardboard

To make templates.

Cotton Puffs

Baby Powder

Soapstone or Sliver of White Soap

Selecting and Preparing the Fabrics

There are 59 different fabrics found in the color palette for the Window of Peace quilt. The large number of colors in a wide variety of hues is necessary in order to obtain subtle shadings in the flowers and to give depth to the quilt. The slight changes in hue, as well as the light bouncing off of some colors, serve to achieve an overall illuminated effect in the quilt. The viewers feel as if they are actually seeing the light coming through the window. Though there are numerous colors, the black leading and the arrangement and balance of the fabrics serve to hold the overall design of the quilt together.

Included in the instructions is a chart listing the colors used for the ''glass.'' Each color has been assigned a number. This number also will be found in each section of the design requiring that color, much like the system used in paint-by-number pictures. You should be able to approximate the look of the quilt on the cover by using this system, though it will be nearly impossible to duplicate it due to differences in, and availability of, fabrics.

Creating Your Own Color

Finding and purchasing all the different colors necessary could prove to be a difficult task. Consider, as an alternative, dyeing fabrics. If this is a process you're familiar with and desire to use, it can give you an almost endless variety of hues. Creating your own colors through the use of dyes, bleaches, and fabric paints can also provide for a variety of effects that cannot usually be achieved with solid colors. Swirls, bands, and smears of color will provide a wide assortment of textures that can imitate the types of glass found in actual stained-glass work.

Several different approaches may be taken to develop your own interpretation of the designs given. Your choice of colors is one way to achieve this personal touch. First, you'll need to decide on a color scheme. A color wheel may be useful in this step (see Diagram 2).

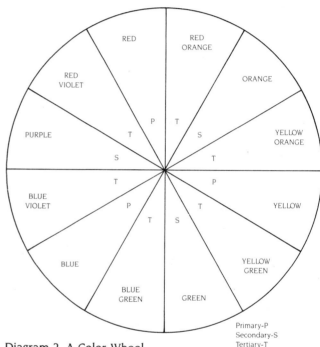

Diagram 2. A Color Wheel

You can choose a monochromatic color scheme. This is the use of one color, with variations being made in the shades and intensities of that color. Using all reds for the flowers would be an example of this. Many variations in color from the palest pink to the deepest maroon could be used.

Using a complementary color scheme is another possible option. Complementary colors are those found opposite each other on the color wheel. Orange and blue, green and red, and purple and yellow are pairs of complementary colors. This type of color scheme will add a diversity that is not found in a monochromatic scheme. Variety may also be added by choosing related colors. These are the colors that are found next to each other on one side of the color wheel. Of course, the most variety will be achieved by using the total range of available colors, but you must be careful to keep the design of the quilt balanced.

When choosing colors, you'll need to consider the amount of each color to be used in the design. If you wish, you can decide to have one color dominate, while the other colors are used to complement it; or you may use an equal amount of each color.

Whatever combination you decide to use, it is important that the final product be balanced and pleasing to the eye. For example, don't put all of one color to one side of the quilt or to one side of an individual block, as this will create an imbalance in the design.

If you're unsure of which colors to use, or you would like to get a better idea of how a fabric will look in a stained-glass quilt, there are several things you can try. Try holding a piece of fabric up to a window or a light box to help you visualize the effect of light on the various colors. The natural light of the window will give you a truer representation of color, as the artificial light of the light box tends to create more distortion in the colors.

Another way to experiment with different color schemes requires the use of colored pencils, watercolors, or crayons. Though not an exact match to fabric colors, this technique will still be useful in determining your color choices. To use this method, place a piece of tracing paper over the pattern. Now, paint or draw with various colors on this paper. Using this method keeps the original pattern free from markings and saves the time required to do multiple sketches of the same design.

Cotton Rather Than a Blend

Color is not the only property you'll need to be concerned with when selecting fabrics. The fiber content of the fabric will also need to be a consideration.

Generally speaking, 100-percent cotton fabric is best to use when doing this type of appliqué. There are several reasons for this. Cotton ravels less than most synthetics, an important factor since many of the pieces in this quilt will be small, and only slightly over ⅛" (3 mm) of the edge of a piece will be covered by the leading.

In addition, cotton fabric is more stable and does not tend to stretch out of shape as quickly as some of the blends. The surface of the cotton also produces less slipping against the backing fabric than blends.

Another advantage of cotton is that when the leading is applied, the black cotton will keep a crease better, and will be easier to appliqué, than a blend.

Perhaps the only disadvantage to the use of cotton instead of a blend is that cotton tends to wrinkle more than most blends.

A final factor to consider when choosing between the use of 100-percent cotton or a blend is the intensity of the color in the final product. Considering how the color will wash out may make a difference in your selection of fabrics. Most blends tend to be thinner, and therefore appear more washed out when light is coming through the quilt. Cotton fabrics are thicker and do not have as strong a tendency to do this; therefore the final product will seem to have stronger colors.

Preparing the Fabric

Once the fabric choices are complete, all fabric must be prepared prior to beginning any cutting or stitching. Most fabrics, especially 100-percent cotton, will shrink with washing. **It is important that shrinkage take place before the fabric is used in a quilt.** All fabric *must* be preshrunk prior to use. You can accomplish this by washing the fabric in the same manner in which the final product will be washed.

Prewashing serves another purpose in preparing the fabric for the quilt: It's a way of checking the fabric for colorfastness. When prewashing fabrics, it is best to wash each piece of fabric separately. If the color runs or washes out, rewash the fabric until the fading stops. If you're unsure whether a dark fabric is still losing color, wash it with a small piece of light-colored fabric. In this way, any color lost from the dark fabric will show on the light fabric.

If a color does not become fast, it is possible to try and set the color. This can be done by boiling the fabric in the mixture of one cup of vinegar in one gallon of water for about ten minutes. The fabric should then be thoroughly rinsed. If color continues to fade, this process may be repeated using approximately one-third of a cup of salt in place of the vinegar. Fabric should then be thoroughly rinsed and washed as normal. On occasion, you'll find a fabric that continues to lose color after repeated washings and attempts to set the color. In cases such as this, the fabric should be discarded. This will prevent any chance of later color fading that would spoil an already completed quilt.

Materials List

Black cotton. You'll need 6 yards (5.5 meters) for bias, borders, and binding for the quilt.

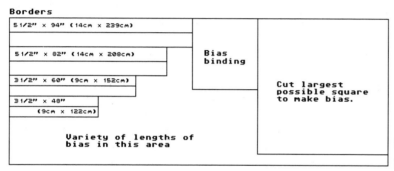

Borders

5 1/2" x 94" (14cm x 239cm)	
5 1/2" x 82" (14cm x 208cm)	**Bias binding**
3 1/2" x 60" (9cm x 152cm)	
3 1/2" x 48" (9cm x 122cm)	**Cut largest possible square to make bias.**
Variety of lengths of bias in this area	

Suggested layout for 3½ yards (3 meters)
Remainder of fabric to be used for bias

Bleached muslin or white cotton. You'll need 9⅝ yards (9 meters) for the foundations of the blocks and the backing of the quilt. Cut the long lengths needed for the backing before cutting any squares.

44" x 98" (112cm x 249cm)	22" x 98" (56cm x 249cm)
	22" x 98" (56cm x 249cm)

5 1/2 yards (5 meters)

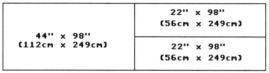

41" x 53" (104cm x 134.5cm)

b	b	b	b	b	a	a
b	b	b	b	b	a	a
b	b	b	b	a	a	a	a

4 1/8 yards (4 meters)

(a) Eight 11" x 13" (28cm x 33cm) blocks
(b) Fourteen 13" x 13" (33cm x 33cm) blocks

Batting. You'll need at least 84" × 96" (213 cm × 244 cm). It's best to use a relatively low-loft batting, as there will already be three layers of fabric in the quilt. This results from the need to use a foundation on which to appliqué the bias and glass pieces.

Various amounts of all of the assorted colors listed. In some cases, very small amounts are needed—you may have sufficient amounts available in a scrap bag. In other cases, larger pieces are needed. As an example, look at the pattern for the rainbow. Though the total amount of fabric required is not large, enough fabric will be needed to have sufficient length. The curved pieces of fabric for the rainbow will be narrow, but long. Therefore, a longer length of fabric will need to be purchased, even though some of it may not be used. In cases such as this, cut the large pieces first in order to ensure adequate fabric. If possible, it is also helpful to purchase "fat quarters" when ¼ yard (0.25 meter) is called for. These quarters measure 18" × 22" (46 cm × 56 cm) in contrast to the normal 9" × 44" (23 × 112 cm).

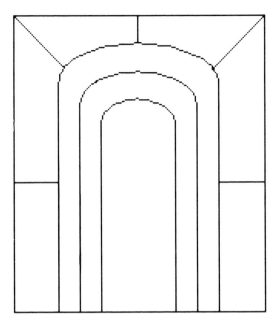

Example-curve of rainbow

Approximate amounts required for each color are given below. All portions of yards and meters that are given are for fabric 44–45 inches (112–114 centimeters) wide. You may find it helpful to tag each piece of fabric in some manner with the number corresponding to that color. These code numbers will be found with the color list. Since many of the colors are quite close, tagging the fabrics will decrease the possibility of mistaking one color for another.

Color Number	Color	Amount English	Amount International
1	Very pale blue	12" × 17"	30 cm × 48 cm
2	Pale blue	½ yard	0.45 meter
3	Medium sky-blue	1 yard	0.9 meter
4	Medium blue	¼ yard	0.25 meter
5	French blue	¼ yard	0.25 meter
6	Cornflower blue	7" × 12"	18 cm × 30 cm
7	Periwinkle blue	½ yard	0.45 meter
8	Dark blue	8" × 10"	21 cm × 26 cm
9	Midnight blue	9" × 17"	23 cm × 48 cm
10	Navy blue	4" × 4"	10 cm × 10 cm
11	Teal-blue	⅓ yard	0.3 meter
12	Turquoise	⅓ yard	0.3 meter
13	Blue-gray	⅓ yard	0.3 meter
14	Pale yellow	12" × 12"	30 cm × 30 cm
15	Light lemon-yellow	3" × 4"	9 cm × 10 cm
16	Light yellow	¼ yard	0.25 meter
17	Medium yellow	⅓ yard	0.3 meter
18	Goldenrod	7" × 8"	18 cm × 21 cm
19	Yellow-orange	5" × 7"	13 cm × 18 cm
20	Yellow-gold	⅛ yard	0.15 meter
21	Orange-gold	½ yard	0.45 meter
22	Gold	15" × 16"	38 cm × 41 cm
23	Spring-green	3" × 4"	9 cm × 10 cm
24	Kelly green	½ yard	0.45 meter
25	Green	4" × 5"	10 cm × 13 cm
26	Dark green	¼ yard	0.25 meter
27	Dark pine-green	5" × 8"	10 cm × 21 cm
28	Forest green	⅓ yard	0.3 meter
29	Apple green	½ yard	0.45 meter
30	Olive	18" × 18"	46 cm × 46 cm
31	Khaki green	5" × 5"	13 cm × 13 cm
32	Light violet	4" × 7"	10 cm × 18 cm
33	Medium violet	6" × 6"	16 cm × 16 cm
34	Medium lilac	⅓ yard	0.3 meter
35	Medium grape	¼ yard	0.25 meter
36	Medium purple	4" × 6"	10 cm × 16 cm
37	Dark purple	7" × 12"	18 cm × 30 cm
38	Pale pink	15" × 22"	38 cm × 56 cm
39	Light pink	10" × 10"	26 cm × 26 cm
40	Medium pink	⅓ yard	0.3 meter
41	Dark raspberry	13" × 13"	33 cm × 33 cm
42	Carnation pink	12" × 12"	30 cm × 30 cm
43	Hot pink	4" × 5"	10 cm × 13 cm
44	Dusty rose	½ yard	0.45 meter
45	Medium rose	10" × 15"	26 cm × 38 cm
46	Light red	4" × 7"	10 cm × 18 cm
47	Medium red	4" × 4"	10 cm × 10 cm
48	Deep red	¼ yard	0.25 meter
49	Medium maroon	4" × 6"	10 cm × 16 cm
50	Dark maroon	8" × 8"	21 cm × 21 cm
51	Dark tan	3" × 6"	9 cm × 16 cm
52	Sepia	3" × 3"	9 cm × 9 cm
53	Dark brown	3" × 4"	9 cm × 10 cm
54	Pale apricot	9" × 12"	23 cm × 30 cm
55	Palest peach	¼ yard	0.25 meter
56	Cream	9" × 12"	23 cm × 30 cm
57	Gray	3" × 5"	9 cm × 13 cm
58	Purplish-gray	4" × 4"	10 cm × 10 cm

Making the Patterns

In order to accommodate the size limitations of this book, all the patterns have been divided into sections and then have been reduced to a smaller scale (about 85-percent the size of the original). Therefore, it will be necessary to match the sections of each design, to make a small drawing, and then to enlarge this drawing to a full-size completed pattern.

Since many areas of the designs are small, you'll need to be careful to achieve proper scale so you'll have sufficient area in each section of the design to appliqué the bias. Do not attempt to execute the designs in fabric without enlarging the drawings. There would not be adequate space in some areas to accommodate a ¼" bias strip.

Since designs in the text may vary in size, it's necessary to have a single method to enlarge the designs, one that will work for any size scale. The method given here will allow you to accomplish this task. You should not allow the process of enlarging the designs to become intimidating, as it can be quite readily performed by using the step-by-step instructions that follow. You should also refer to the special notes that follow the instructions, and it's a good idea to read all the instructions once before beginning the enlarging process.

Step 1

In the pattern section of the text, individual designs are labeled. Most designs will be found in two sections. To make a complete pattern, the sections simply need to be joined by matching the broken lines. First, place a sheet of tracing paper over the first half of the design. Using a pencil, trace all lines of the design,

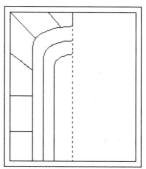

First section traced   Both sections traced

Diagram 3. Tracing a Pattern

including the broken line. Next, place the tracing paper over the second half of the design, matching the broken lines. Finish tracing the design. Diagram 3 illustrates this step.

Step 2

Take the tracing paper away from the book and go over all of the solid lines with a black felt-tip pen. The drawing is now complete and ready to be enlarged.

Step 3

This step will be most important for ensuring the accuracy of the various pattern pieces, so it will be divided into several smaller steps. Enlarging the designs involves making a grid of the reduced-size drawing and a corresponding grid for the full-size pattern. The following list gives the grid necessary to enlarge each design.

Design	Grid to be made	Full-size pattern
Small roses	8 sq. × 8 sq.	8" × 8" (20 cm × 20 cm)
Iris & tulips	10 sq. × 12 sq.	10" × 12" (25 cm × 30 cm)
All other flowers	12 sq. × 12 sq.	12" × 12" (30 cm × 30 cm)
Rose border	8 sq. × 24 sq.	8" × 24" (20 cm × 60 cm)
Extended rose border	8 sq. × 36 sq.	8" × 36" (20 cm × 90 cm)
Center dove motif	24 sq. × 36 sq.	24" × 36" (60 cm × 90 cm)

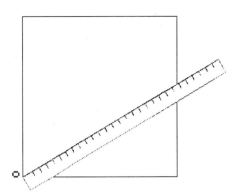

As you can see, both the reduced-size and the full-size grid will have the same number of squares—it's the size of these squares that will differ. The size of the squares in the small grids will depend on the size of your reduced-size drawings. On the full-size grids, one square will always represent 1". You can see in the list above that most of the flowers will be made in a 12" square. This means that the grid will be twelve 1" squares by twelve 1" squares.

As an example, I am going to use a 5" reduced-size drawing and enlarge it to fit a 12" block. This means that the 5" drawing needs to be divided into 12 equal parts before enlarging it to 12". The following steps will accomplish this task. (Note: I will be giving measurements only in inches in the following steps, but the same principles apply to International measurements.)

A. Measure the size of your tracing. Using a right-angle or a T-square, draw a square or rectangle equal to this size. I will be using a 5" × 5" square as an example.

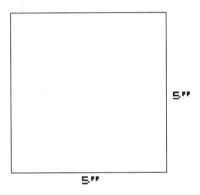

B. Choose the next highest number above the size of your drawing that may be divided easily into the number of squares necessary for your grid. For the example, I want the 5" square divided into 12 equal parts. The next highest number above 5 that is easily divisible by 12 is 6. If I were dividing the square into 8 or 10 parts, for example, the next highest number is either 8 or 10.

C. Place the zero-point of a ruler on the lower left corner of the square, with the ruler positioned on an angle.

D. Maneuver the ruler up and down the line on the right side of the square until the 6" mark of the ruler is on this line.

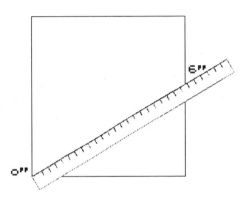

On some drawings, the point that needs to be marked is above the side of the square. This situation is easily handled by extending the side of the square above the top line of the square.

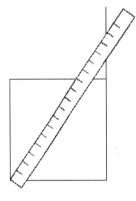

E. Divide the number on the right side of the square by the number of squares needed for the grid, and place a dot at these intervals along the length of the ruler from the zero mark to the right side. In the example, ½" intervals from 0 to 6 give the necessary 12 equal divisions.

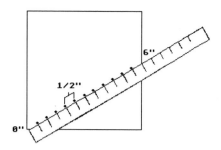

F. With a T-square or right-angle, and using the dots and the bottom line of the square as guidelines, draw the lines of the grid.

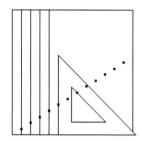

G. Rotate the paper and repeat the process to establish grid lines in the opposite direction.

H. Go over all lines of the grid with the black felt-tip pen so that the grid will show through tracing paper. The grid is now complete. The process just described will work for any size drawing, for any number of divisions in a grid.

Step 4

Draw the large grid. This is easily accomplished by drawing a square equal to the full-size dimensions of the design and placing a grid line at 1" intervals both vertically and horizontally.

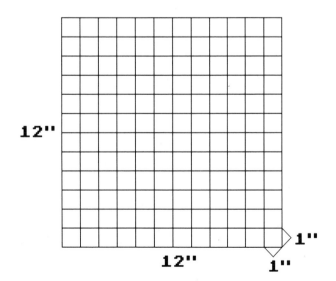

Step 5

Place the tracing of the reduced-size drawing over the small grid and fasten in place.

Step 6

Place a sheet of tracing paper over the large grid, and fasten it in place.

Step 7

Using a pencil, copy what appears in each square of the small grid onto the corresponding square of the large grid. This should be done as precisely as possible to ensure the accuracy of the full-size pattern. An example of this is given in the illustrations that follow.

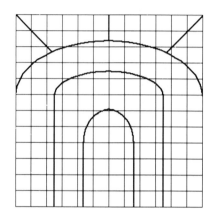

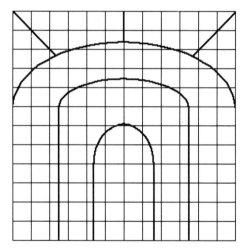

Step 8

When you've finished copying, trace over the enlargement with the black felt-tip pen.

Step 9

If you're using the suggested colors, copy the numbers from the design in the book onto the pattern. With these steps completed, you're now ready to use the pattern.

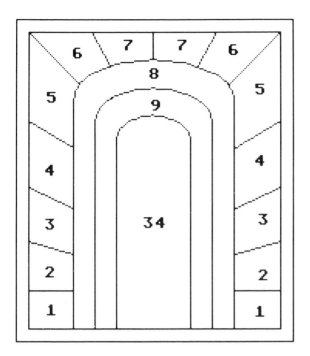

Special Notes

Grids may be reused, and it may not always be necessary to make a new grid for each reduced-size drawing. For example, the grid that was made for the 5" square and divided into 12 parts may be used for any reduced drawing that is 5" and requires 12 divisions to enlarge the design. The 12" full-size grid that was made in the example may be reused for all flower blocks that have a finished size of 12" X 12".

Some blocks in the quilt are rectangular in shape. This will not present a problem when enlarging the designs. Note that the iris and tulip blocks measure 10" X 12". In these cases, the small grid should be divided by 10 in the shorter dimension, and by 12 on the longer side of the rectangle.

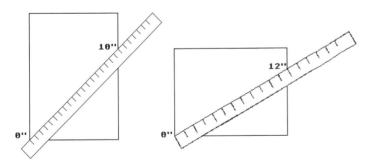

This will give you a grid that's 10 squares X 12 squares. The larger grid is made by constructing a rectangle measuring 10" X 12" and dividing this into 1" increments in both directions.

In most cases, matching the parts of the designs and making one drawing which is then enlarged is the best method to ensure pattern accuracy. However, because of the size of the center panel and the rose borders, it will be easier to enlarge these areas in sections. The sections may then be joined together when the pattern is transferred to the fabric base. This prevents the need for large and cumbersome sheets of paper. The suggested methods of enlarging these parts of the design are given below.

Center panel: This motif consists of 12 sections, each measuring 6" X 12" (see the pattern section of the text). The large grid should be made equal to this size and be divided into 1" increments. The reduced-size drawings should also be divided into 6 square X 12 square grids using the method for rectangles. Each of the 12 sections should then be individually enlarged. These sections are then matched when the design is transferred to the fabric.

The *rose borders* will require a slight alteration in this process. As there are several sizes to the various sections for the borders, the process of enlarging each section separately could become confusing. Therefore, it is suggested that the reduced-size drawings be matched together as shown by the illustrations in the pattern section. These should then be traced so that there is a reduced-size drawing of the complete border. This drawing should then be divided in half, and each half should be enlarged individually. The two halves may be rejoined when the pattern is transferred to the fabric. Using this method, the following grids are necessary:

- Rose border (full size equals 8" X 24")
  Half of the length of the border = 8" X 12"
  Small grid necessary = 8 sq. X 12 sq.
  Large grid necessary = 8" X 12", divided into 1" squares

- Extended rose border (full size equals 8" X 36")
  Half of the length of the border = 8" X 18"
  Small grid necessary = 8 sq. X 18 sq.
  Large grid necessary = 8" X 18", divided into 1" squares

11

Making Bias Strips

Prior to cutting any strips, the large pieces of black fabric that will be needed for the quilt borders should be cut. See steps in assembling quilt top for the sizes needed for these borders. Refer to the materials list for a suggested cutting layout.

Step 1

Cut a square of fabric. This may be any size, but it must be a perfect square. It's best to cut the biggest possible square, as this will provide longer strips of bias which will be required in certain areas of the design.

Step 2

Fold the square in half diagonally; press. This will divide the square of fabric into two equal triangles. Next, open the fabric out and mark a line from point A to point B. A white pencil, soapstone, sliver of white soap, or tailor's chalk is best for marking lines on black fabric.

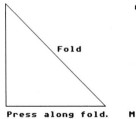
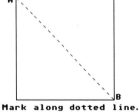

Press along fold.   Mark along dotted line.

Step 3

Measure and mark lines every ¾" (1.9 cm), parallel to diagonal line AB.

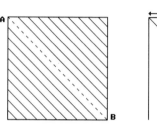
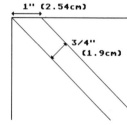

Step 4

Cut strips along lines.

Step 5

Press over approximately 3/16" (5 mm) on one side of strip.

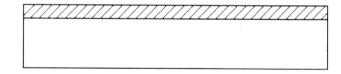

Step 6

Fold over other side of strip, with this edge overlapping the first edge. Press.

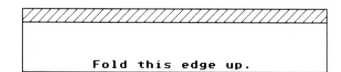

Fold this edge up.

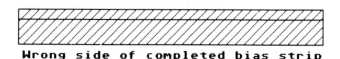

Wrong side of completed bias strip

This will give a finished bias strip about ¼" (6 mm) wide. Repeat this process with all strips. Strips of varying lengths are now ready for appliqué. It is important to save the longest strips for the long lines in the designs. This will prevent unnecessary splicing that detracts from the overall appearance of the quilt.

In general, most individual squares will require between 4–5½ yards (3.6–4.95 meters) of bias to complete the appliqué. The small roses require approximately 3 yards (2.7 meters). The rose border will require about 42 yards (37.8 meters). The dove and rainbow will require approximately 20 yards (1.8 meters). The total requirement for ¼" (6 mm) bias is approximately 184 yards (166 meters). Think of this amount as a guide for how much bias to make. The amount can vary depending on how much the fabric is stretched, how much waste takes place as a result of pieces of bias that are too short, and a variety of other factors.

In addition to the ¼" bias, you'll need approximately 5½ yards (5 meters) of ⅜" (9 mm) bias for around the dove and rainbow, and 7 yards (6.3 meters) of ½" (1.2 cm) bias to assemble the blocks. It's easiest to make only part of the bias, then do some appliqué, and then return to making bias as needed. This prevents the task from becoming monotonous.

How to Make Continuous Bias Binding

A continuous bias binding is a good time-saver when making the binding for a quilt. It allows you to sew two long seams in place of the many short ones. You can also choose to use this method when making the leading for the quilt since you may find it more convenient to have a long roll of binding instead of many short pieces. The disadvantage of this method is that you'll be sewing seams that are not necessary and will not be used. If continuous bias is used for leading, it's a good idea to cut away all seams prior to using for appliqué. This decreases the bulk, and the leading is more attractive when no seams in the bias are exposed.

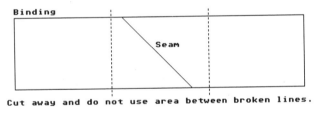

Cut away and do not use area between broken lines.

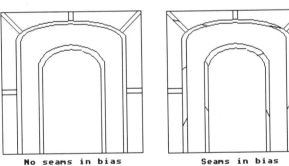

No seams in bias   Seams in bias

Diagram 4. Example of Bias With and Without Seams

Step 1

Cut square of black cotton. A square that's 24–25 inches (60–62 centimeters) will be needed to make the approximately ten yards of binding that will be necessary to bind the quilt.

Step 2

Fold square in half diagonally and press. This will divide the square of fabric into two equal triangles. Next, open fabric and cut along pressed line from point A to point B.

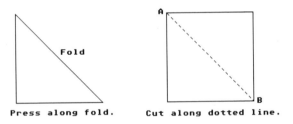

Press along fold.   Cut along dotted line.

Step 3

With the right sides facing, stitch the two triangles together as illustrated. Use a ¼" (6 mm) seam allowance. Press the seam.

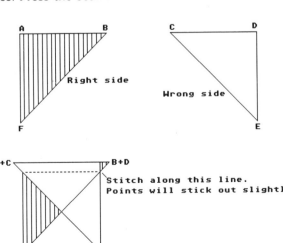

Stitch along this line.
Points will stick out slightly.

The fabric is now in the shape of a parallelogram.

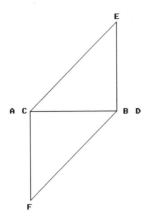

Step 4

Measure and mark strips parallel to the diagonal side of the parallelogram.

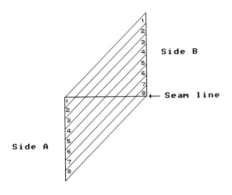

For binding the quilt, these strips should be 1½" (38 cm) wide. This will give a finished ¼" (6mm) double-thickness binding. The strips may be cut wider if a wider binding is desired, but be certain to allow extra yardage. If using this method to make bias for leading, mark ¾" (1.9 cm) wide strips. (Note: If this method is being used for bias leading, you can choose not to proceed past this step. Strips may be cut apart now to use for leading. You can choose to continue with the steps if a continuous roll of bias is desired, but seams will need to be cut away before using bias, as noted earlier in the text.)

Step 5

With right sides together, and sides matched unevenly as shown in the illustration, stitch side A to side B. Allow ¼" (6 mm) seam. When this stitching is completed, the fabric will have formed a tube.

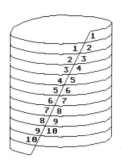

Step 6

Following the marked lines, cut tube to form a continuous bias strip.

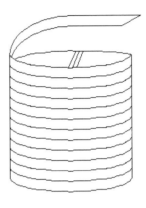

Step 7

If bias is to be used as binding, fold strip in half along the entire length, pressing as you fold. This is now a double-thickness bias binding. The advantage of this type of binding is that it is stronger so will not wear out as quickly as a single-fold bias. The bias binding is now ready to be applied to the quilt. If bias is being used for leading, follow the instructions given earlier in the text for pressing bias strips.

How to Appliqué the Designs

Step 1

Cut foundation for block from bleached muslin or white cotton. The 12" (30.5 cm) blocks will require a 13" X 13" (33 cm X 33 cm) backing. When measuring the fabric, draw seam lines at 12" (30.5 cm) and cutting line at 13" (33 cm) as shown in the illustration.

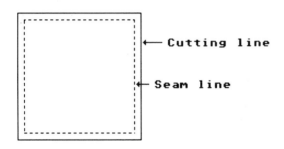

The 10" X 12" (25.4 cm X 30.5 cm) blocks will require a foundation that measures 11" X 13" (28 cm X 33 cm). The seam lines will be marked at 10" X 12" (25.4 cm X 30.5 cm); the cutting lines, at 11" X 13" (28 X 33 cm). To make the center portion of the quilt as shown, cut a rectangle 41" X 53" (104.1 cm X 134.6 cm). Mark the seam lines at 40" X 52" (101.6 cm X 132 cm). The dove and rainbow, the small roses, and the rose borders will be appliquéd on this backing. The finished size of this center portion will be 40" X 52" (101.6 cm X 132 cm).

Step 2

Transfer designs from patterns to fabric using one of the following methods.

Method A

Position the pattern in the center of the fabric and secure with pins, or, if you prefer, use tape. The outer line of the pattern will be on the seam line you marked in Step 1. Slip dressmaker's carbon between pattern and fabric. Trace the design onto the fabric.

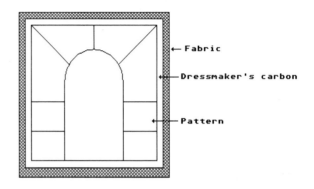

Method B

Tape the pattern on a window, on a light box, or on top of a glass table. Center the fabric over the pattern. The seam line marked on the fabric should match the outer line of the pattern.

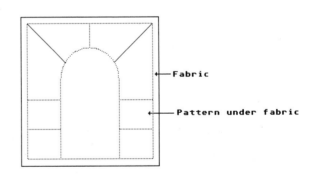

The light of the light box, sunlight coming through the window, or light from a lamp under the glass table will provide sufficient lighting for the pattern to show through the fabric. A piece of white paper behind the tracing paper pattern will help darken the lines of the pattern, allowing for easier tracing. Using a pencil, trace the pattern onto the fabric.

Step 3

If you're using the colors given in the text, number the sections on the fabric to match the numbers of the colors on the patterns. Do not number any sections that will be left white, as the numbers in the white sections will not be covered with another fabric and any markings will show on the finished product. These sections are easily determined. All white areas are numbered 59 on the patterns. The backing for the block is now ready to be used.

Step 4

Again using the paper patterns, trace the individual shapes found in the designs onto the appropriate fabric colors. Pieces should be cut to the exact size of the pattern. Do *not* add ¼" (6 mm) seams. These pieces of fabric will be the glass. It is most convenient and time saving to cut all pieces of one color to be used in one design before proceeding to the next color. The white areas of the designs will not require glass pieces. These areas will be left with the white cotton showing through.

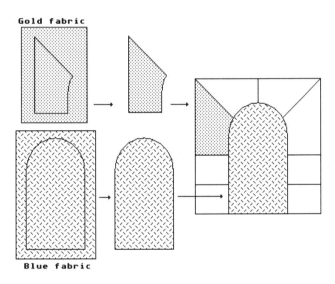

If adjacent areas require the same color, glass may be cut as one large piece. This prevents unnecessary raw edges and allows easier stitching. The pieces should be marked with lines where the bias is to be placed (see Diagram 5). There are also a few places where colors are marked in spaces that will not actually need to be filled with glass. These spaces were simply marked for consistency, but because they are so small, the bias coming together here will cover any space where a piece of glass would be placed (see Diagram 6).

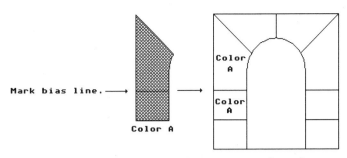

Diagram 5. Marking Bias on Adjacent Pieces of a Color

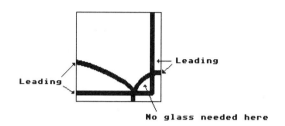

Diagram 6. Small Areas in Designs

Step 5

Baste the pieces onto the appropriate sections of the foundation for the block. Use a long running stitch about ¼" (6 mm) in from the edge of the fabric.

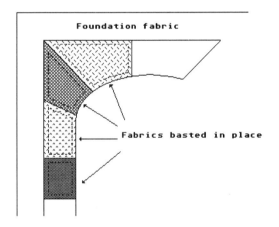

Complete the basting of all pieces of the block prior to beginning any leading.

Step 6

In this type of appliqué, bias leading is placed over the line where the pieces of glass meet.

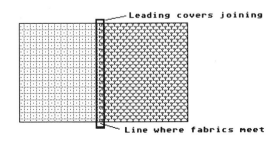

It's important that the bias be applied so all ends of the bias are hidden. Therefore, it must be appliquéd over the lines in a definite order. The diagrams below will help illustrate this point.

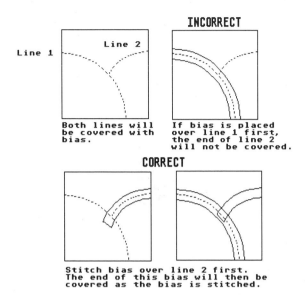

Line 1 ----- Line 2

Both lines will be covered with bias.

INCORRECT

If bias is placed over line 1 first, the end of line 2 will not be covered.

CORRECT

Stitch bias over line 2 first. The end of this bias will then be covered as the bias is stitched.

As a reference, the pattern for the large rose has been lettered. These letters show the order in which you appliqué the bias over the pattern lines. (Note: The letters start with A, continue through Z, and then start again with AA. The center portion is not marked; directions for it are given in a later illustration.) It will be helpful if you stitch this block first. After becoming acquainted with the technique through this design, you'll find it easier to complete the other designs by determining the proper order in which to place the bias.

In the large rose pattern, as with most designs, work will begin toward the edge of the block and move toward the center. Once you've studied the pattern, it will become clear that all of the bias pieces may be appliquéd completely until reaching the center of the design. At that point, some pieces will need to be appliquéd only partially. Spaces must be left until all ends of the strips of bias can be stitched under an adjoining piece. Diagram 7 should clarify this point.

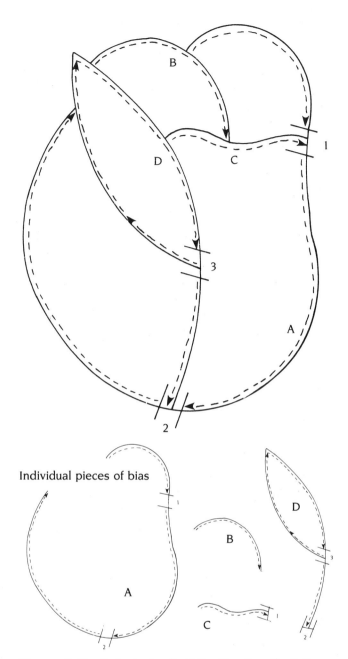

Individual pieces of bias

Diagram 7. The Order to Appliqué the Bias Over the Pattern Lines

To complete the center of the block, first stitch bias piece A, leaving openings at points 1 and 2. Next, stitch bias piece B. Stitch piece C, tucking end under bias piece A at point 1. Complete stitching bias piece A over end of piece C. Stitch bias piece D beginning at point 3 and following the direction of the arrow, ending at point 2. Form point as described later in the directions for the appliqué. Piece D will overlap itself at point 3. The end of piece D will be tucked under piece A at point 2. Complete stitching piece A over the end of piece D.

Special Notes About Sewing Bias

1. On curved lines in the design, always sew the inner curves prior to the outer curves. Stitching in this order will help to prevent puckering of the bias. The reason for this is that since the outer curve is longer than the inner curve, if it is stitched first, the bias may be stretched. This will leave the bias too long for the inner curve, and it will need to be tucked to fit the space. Stitching the inner curve first will prevent this—the shorter inner curve will then be smooth, and the bias may be stretched to fit the longer outer curve.

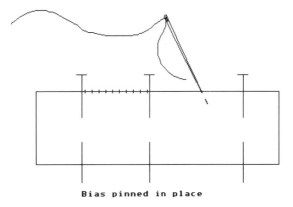

Bias pinned in place

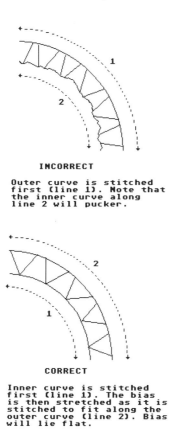

INCORRECT

Outer curve is stitched first (line 1). Note that the inner curve along line 2 will pucker.

CORRECT

Inner curve is stitched first (line 1). The bias is then stretched as it is stitched to fit along the outer curve (line 2). Bias will lie flat.

2. To appliqué the bias, use a single strand of black thread and an invisible hemming stitch. To do the hemming stitch, the needle should just be caught in the edge of the bias. The longer part of the stitch will be under the fabric.

Stitches should be made approximately every ⅛" (3 mm). On points and sharp curves, the stitches should be closer so the fabric will be held in place.

3. The curves in some designs are quite sharp, and points will need to be made in others. In these situations, handle the bias as follows.

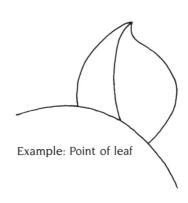

Example: Point of leaf

On the leaf above, the bias will come to a point. This point in the bias will be achieved by mitering the bias. As shown in the following illustration, for the most attractive look, this miter should extend from the point of the leaf rather than to the side of the point.

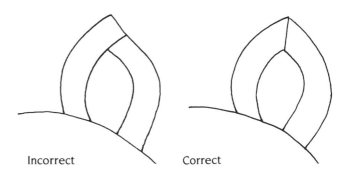

Incorrect   Correct

In order to achieve the proper miter, take the following steps:

A. Stitch the inner curve of the leaf up to the point of the leaf, and then a few stitches past the point.

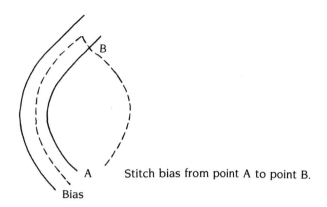

Bias

Stitch bias from point A to point B.

B. Fold bias straight back at point B.

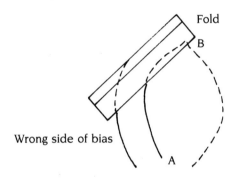

Fold

Wrong side of bias

C. Fold bias forward on a 45-degree angle, following line C between points X and Y.

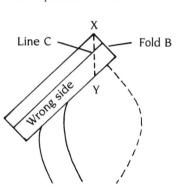

Line C — Fold B

Wrong side

Bias folded forward along C

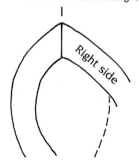

Right side

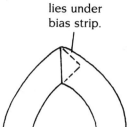

Fold of fabric lies under bias strip.

D. After blind-stitching along fold C, continue on with the stitching of the inside curve of the leaf.

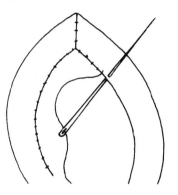

E. When the inside curve is done, stitch the outer curve, taking a few extra stitches to secure the point.

4. A completed block will have raw edges of both the bias and the glass pieces showing around the edge of the block. These will be covered when the blocks are assembled and the leading is appliquéd over the seams. Leave the basting on these edges until the joining leading is applied.

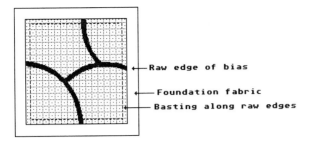

— Raw edge of bias

— Foundation fabric

— Basting along raw edges

5. This note pertains only to the center medallion. The bias around the dove and rainbow section and extending between the small rose blocks and rose borders should be ⅜" (9 mm) rather than the standard ¼" (6 mm). This bias can be made by cutting strips ⅞" (2.2 cm) wide and then continuing in the normal fashion to make strips for appliqué. If necessary, to obtain the needed length, strips cut on the straight of the grain rather than bias strips may be used in this step as there are no curves involved.

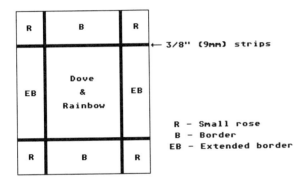

← 3/8" (9mm) strips

R – Small rose
B – Border
EB – Extended border

Setting of the Quilt

The quilt was assembled according to Diagram 8. It uses all of the designs found in this text. To create the quilt, you'll need to make the center medallion consisting of the dove and rainbow enclosed by the rose borders. The following blocks will also be needed:

- One each of the fire lily, gentian, poppy, pansy, saffron, columbine, orchid, daffodil, morning glory, and bleeding heart.
- Four tulip blocks.
- Two iris blocks and two reverse iris blocks.
- Two large rose blocks and two reverse large rose blocks.

The reverse blocks are made simply by turning the patterns over from left to right so that the reverse pattern becomes a mirror image of the original.

You can choose to use this setting, or any other combination of blocks, depending on your individual taste. For example, you might choose to repeat only one or two of the flowers rather than using a different flower for each block.

When deciding on a setting other than that given, it's important to note that not all blocks are of the same size. The iris and tulip blocks are 10" × 12" (25.4 cm × 30.5 cm). The other floral blocks are 12" square (30.5 cm × 30.5 cm). If you decide to make the center rainbow and the dove with the border of roses, you'll need to choose two rectangular and two square blocks

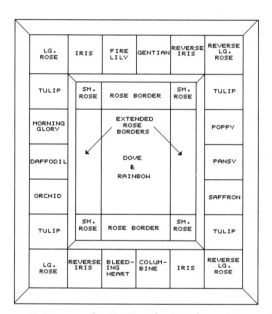

Diagram 8. Diagram for Setting the Window of Peace Quilt

for the width of the quilt. Two rectangular and three square blocks will be necessary for the length of the quilt. Four square blocks will be needed for the corners of the quilt.

On the pages following Diagram 8, you'll find complete instructions for assembling the quilt top.

Steps in Assembling the Quilt Top

Step 1

Cut two strips of black fabric 3½" × 48" (9 cm × 122 cm.), and two strips 3½" × 60" (9 cm × 122 cm.). These strips will form the black border around the inner medallion of the quilt.

Step 2

Measure 40" (101.6 cm) on one long side of each of the two shorter strips, beginning at the center and measuring 20" (50.8 cm) in each direction. Mark points with white marking pencil.

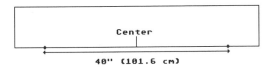

With right sides together, pin short strips to opposite sides of center medallion, matching points on strips to points ¼" (6 mm) from the edge of the medallion. The strips will extend past the sides of the medallion. This is to allow enough extra fabric to make mitered corners on the border. Stitch ¼" (6 mm) seam between points. Press, with seams pressed toward border.

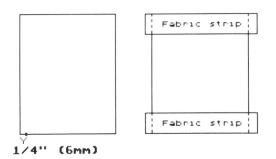

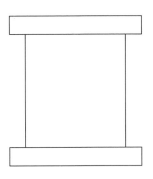

Step 3

Repeat Step 2 with the fabric strips for the longer sides of the medallion, measuring 52" (132 cm) on these strips (26" or 66 cm in each direction from the center), and then attaching them to the medallion in the same way as the shorter strips. The piece should now appear as illustrated below.

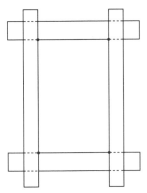

Strips are stitched between points only.

The longer strips are now overlapping the shorter strips, but they aren't attached to the shorter ones. Ends of all four strips past the marked points are loose at this time.

Step 4

At points where stitching ends, fold each strip back at a 45-degree angle. Press.

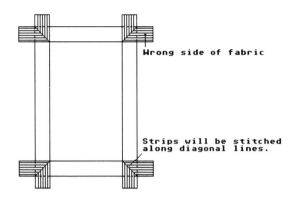

Wrong side of fabric

Strips will be stitched along diagonal lines.

With right sides together, pin ends of strips together along the crease formed by pressing the strips. Stitch along this crease line. Repeat for the other three corners. Trim seams to ¼" (6 mm). Press seams to one side. Mitered corners of the border should now look like the illustration below.

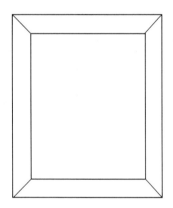

Step 5

Make 18 bias strips, each ½" (12 mm) wide, and each a minimum of 12" (30.5 cm) long. Follow instructions given earlier for making bias strips, except strips should initially be cut 1" (2.54 cm) wide. One-quarter inch (approximately 6 mm) should then be pressed over on each side to make the finished strip ½" (12 mm) wide.

Step 6

Stitch blocks 1 to 4 together, including only the backing fabric in the seam. Stitch along line shown in illustration. The edges of the colored fabrics will be loose at this time. These edges will be covered in the next step when the bias is appliquéd, rather than being incorporated in the seams. This will help reduce the bulkiness of the seams. Trim seams to ¼" (6 mm) and press to one side.

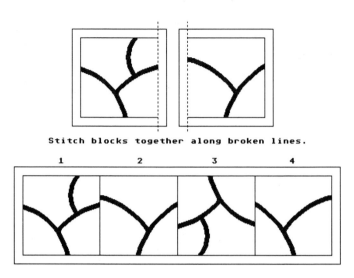

Stitch blocks together along broken lines.

Step 7

Appliqué ½" (12 mm) bias strips over the seams.

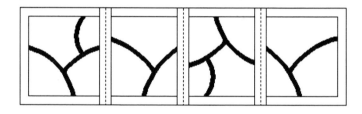

Step 8

Stitch a 1" (2.54 cm) wide strip of black to each end of the row of blocks, stitching in ¼" (6 mm) from edge of glass pieces so that the edges are encased in the seam. Press seam toward black fabric.

24

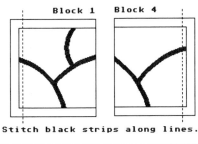

Block 1   Block 4

Stitch black strips along lines.

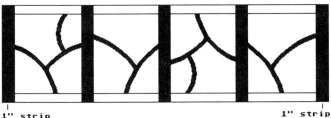

1" strip   1" strip

Step 9
Repeat steps 6, 7, and 8 with blocks 5 through 8.

Step 10
Stitch strip with blocks 1–4 to the top of the quilt, stitching in ¼" (6 mm) from the edge of the colored fabrics so all layers of the block are encased in the seam. Trim excess fabric. Stitch strip with blocks 5–8 to the bottom of the quilt. Press seams toward black borders.

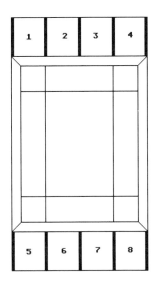

Step 11
Stitch blocks 9–15 together using the same process as in steps 6 and 7. Do not add black strips to ends of rows. Make sure that all blocks are right side up.

Step 12
Repeat steps 6 and 7 for blocks 16–22.

Step 13
Using the same process as described in step 10, stitch strip of blocks 9–15 to the left side of the quilt. Stitch blocks 16–22 to the right side of the quilt. Press seams toward the black border.

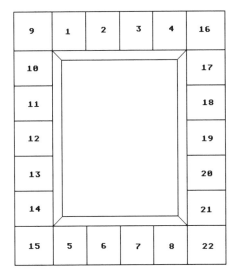

Step 14
The last step in assembly is to add a 5" (12.7 cm) wide black border. Cut two strips of black 5½" × 82" (14 cm × 208 cm), and two strips 5½" × 94" (14 cm × 239 cm). Measure 70" (178 cm) on one long side of each short strip, beginning in the center and measuring half the distance out to each side. Repeat this on the longer strips, measuring 82" (208 cm). Mark these points with a white pencil. Proceed from here following steps 2–4 until the border is attached and the corners are mitered. Press. The quilt top is now complete.

Preparing the Quilt Back

The back of the quilt uses white cotton. This fabric will allow more light through the quilt than a darker fabric would, maintaining the effect of light shining through a window. Three strips of fabric, each 98" (249 cm) long will be required for the backing. One strip should be the complete width of fabric 44–45 inches (115 centimeters) wide minus the selvages. The other two strips should measure 22" (56 cm) wide. Using these measurements, the backing will extend 3" to 4" (7.6 cm to 10 cm) beyond the quilt top on all sides. This allows for ease in the quilt as the quilting is done. Extra ease will help prevent any possibility of the edge of the quilt and the edge of the backing not matching when the quilting is completed. Any excess amount of backing will be trimmed later.

Using ⅝" (15 mm) seams, stitch the three strips together, with the widest strip in the center. Press seams toward the center.

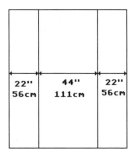

It's important to use three strips rather than two for the backing. There are for two reasons for this. First, the backing will be stronger with the stress divided between two seams. Second, a seam to either side on the backing of the quilt will not tend to be as apparent on the front of the quilt as a seam down the center.

Basting the Quilt

The next step in the process of making the quilt is basting together the top, batting, and backing. The steps to complete this process are given below.

Step 1

Mark midpoints on all sides of quilt top and quilt back. Safety pins are easiest to use.

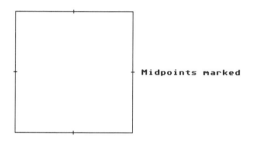

Midpoints marked

Step 2

Make sure that both the quilt top and the backing are carefully pressed. It is useful to baste the seams of the backing flat before pressing and to leave this stitching in until the layers are basted together. This will keep these long seams in place. It is important that this final pressing be thorough and that no wrinkles are present on the quilt or the backing. Remember, quilts may not be pressed after the batting is in place.

Step 3

The method used in the next step depends largely on personal preference. There are several ways to handle the layers in order to do the basting. You may use a tile floor, a carpeted floor, a table, or a wooden frame as a surface for the basting. Whichever method you choose, the backing is the first layer attached in preparation for basting. First, lay the backing perfectly flat, wrong side up.

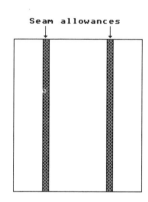

Seam allowances

Then tape it to the floor or table, or pin it to the carpet. If you used any of these methods, proceed to step 4.

Instead of the above methods, I prefer to stretch the backing in a wooden frame. The frame can easily be made with one-by-fours and C-clamps. The boards will need to be long enough so that the inside measurements of the frame will be equal to the measurements of the quilt. Measure the width of the quilt on two of the boards and the length of the quilt on the other two boards. Next, clamp the boards together at the four corners using C-clamps. Using a right-angle or a T-square will ensure that the frame forms a true square, with each corner being a right angle, when clamped together.

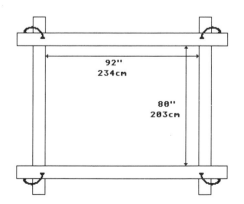

92"
234cm

80"
203cm

Place the completed frame on four high-back chairs as shown in the illustration. Matching centers of boards and sides of backing, pin backing to frame using push pins. Since the backing is larger than the finished quilt, it will extend onto the boards. Place push pins only in the edge of the fabric so they won't create holes in the parts of the fabric that are actually part of the quilt.

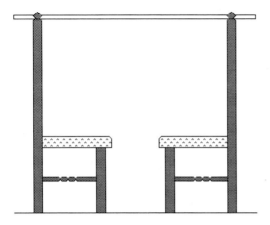

After the backing is on the frame, you'll complete the rest of the basting in the same fashion as the other methods. Three important advantages of using the wooden frame are:

• The backing remains quite flat with no possibility of wrinkles
• You can reach both above and below the quilt while basting
• The quilt is raised off the floor

Step 4

When you've completely secured the backing by any of the above methods, lay batting on top of the backing and smooth it out as necessary. Batting should lie flat and extend somewhat past the dimensions of the quilt.

Step 5

Finally, place the quilt face up on the batting. Match the midpoints of the top with the midpoints of the back. Pin in place.

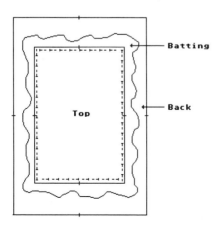

Step 6

You should baste every 4–6 inches (10–15 centimeters) to hold the layers firmly together. Use a light-colored thread, as darker threads sometimes have a tendency to lose some color on the fabrics. A curved household needle is also useful, but don't use a large needle since it may leave holes in the fabric. When basting on the floor or other flat surface, a spoon can be helpful for pushing the fabric down while bringing the needle back up through all the layers. To begin basting, start in the center and work out to the sides of the quilt in a sun-ray pattern.

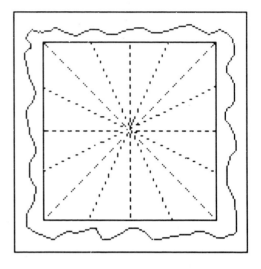

Step 7

Now baste horizontal lines every 4–6 inches (10–15 centimeters), and then vertical lines every 4–6 inches (10–15 centimeters).

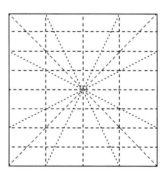

Step 8

Basting is now complete. All pins and/or tape may now be removed. If you used a frame, take the quilt off of the frame. It's a good idea at this time to fold the excess backing over to the front edge of the top and baste it in place. This protects the edges of the fabric and the batting while you're quilting.

Quilting Tips

- Always thread the needle before cutting the thread from the spool. Because the thread is twisted, it's easier to insert the end while it's still attached to the spool than to try using a loose thread that has untwisted. This also helps to prevent tangling and unwanted knotting of the thread as the stitching is done.

- Use short (18–20 inches or 45–51 centimeters) lengths of thread for both appliqué and quilting. Although you might be tempted to take longer lengths in order to decrease the number of times you have to thread the needle or the number of times a thread must be ended, longer lengths of thread could lead to problems. There may be more knots and tangling of the thread with longer lengths, and there will be excess wearing of the thread as it is repeatedly pulled through the fabric. There's no need to have the strength of your thread jeopardized before the quilt is even completed.

- As a time-saving move, thread a number of needles at one time. Many people, especially those who have more difficulty seeing as evening approaches, like to do this in daylight. This enables them to continue quilting into the evening hours. Do not cut thread between needles. Simply leave the thread attached to the spool with all the needles hanging on it. As needed, pull out a length of thread and a needle and then clip.

- If you're right-handed, it's easier to quilt from right to left. If you're left-handed, quilt from left to right. If you have to quilt in a different direction, which sometimes can't be avoided in certain areas of the design, it's easier to quilt toward yourself. You'll have better results if you try to quilt no farther than an arm's length away.

- Running the thread through beeswax (available at any fabric shop) gives it strength and helps prevent tangles.

- Do not have the quilt fastened too tautly while it's in a frame or hoop. There needs to be enough stretching so it has neither puffiness nor wrinkles, but there also needs to be some flexibility in the quilt. A little bit of bounce will allow better handling of the quilt. It will be easier to get the needle through the three layers and allow for smoother, more even stitching.

- Ten to twelve stitches per inch is considered average and acceptable for quilting, but it is more important, especially if you're a beginner, to work on consistency in the size of stitches. Even if you don't achieve your goal for whatever number of stitches per inch, consistent, even stitches will be more attractive than stitches of varying sizes. Smaller stitching will come with practice. You'll also become accustomed to the smaller needles used in quilting.

- Never leave pins or needles in your quilt for long periods of time. This can cause dark spots on the fabric.

- If you come to the end of a design and you have a length of the thread left, run the thread through the batting to the closest nearby design. Then resume quilting. This will prevent extra knotting or ending of threads.

- Test all marking instruments, such as the soapstone, on individual fabrics prior to use on the quilt to make sure that markings will wash out. This ensures that the markings can be removed from fabrics after the quilting is complete.

Marking the Quilting Lines

If you quilt close to the leading, no marking will be needed in those areas. If you quilt approximately ¼" (6 mm) away from the leading, ¼" (6 mm) masking tape works nicely to mark a quilting line. Simply place one edge of the tape against the leading and quilt along the opposite edge. Then pull the tape away from the fabric. This width of masking tape is now available at many quilting supply stores, as well as hardware and paint stores.

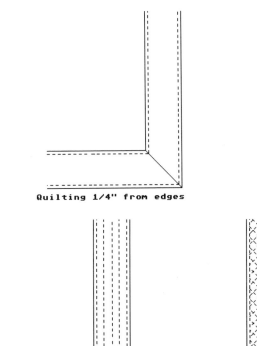
Quilting 1/4" from edges

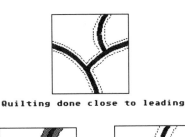
Quilting done close to leading

Masking tape is placed against lead-ing. Quilt close to tape.

Quilting after masking tape has been re-moved.

Two variations of designs to add texture

Remember to take the masking tape off immediately after quilting to avoid leaving a residue that could cause damage to the fabric.

The marking on the narrow border can also be accomplished using only masking tape. This 3" (7.6 cm) border is simply quilted ¼" (6 mm) in from both edges. These lines are easily marked with the ¼" (6 mm) masking tape. To add texture to the border, you may quilt more lines, crosshatching, or other allover or background designs to fill in the smooth space. This marking can also easily be achieved by using a variety of widths of masking tape.

The outer border is quilted ¼" (6 mm) in from the inner edge and ½" (12 mm) in from the outer edge of the border. These lines are marked with masking tape. The more intricate part of the design of the outer border will require more marking than can be achieved with masking tape. This marking will be done with a template, cotton puffs, baby powder, and a soapstone or a sliver of white soap; the marking will wash out when the quilting is complete. In most quilts, the marking is done after the piecing is complete and before the three layers are basted together. Since the white markings may easily brush off the black border, and because this border is the last area to be quilted, you may want to delay the marking until it's time to quilt this area.

The first step in marking the design is to make a template from the pattern for the quilted rose (all the patterns appear in the last section of this book). You may find it more convenient to make the template for the twining separately. The rose can be done by tracing it from the book and then transferring the design to the template material. Template material may be a thin cardboard, such as is found in file folders, or a sheet of acetate, which is available at art supply stores. After you draw the template, punch holes along each line of the design. The holes can easily be made with an ice pick or by stitching over the lines with a large needle on an unthreaded sewing machine. Make sure that there are holes at the end of each line as well as at any points (see Diagram 9).

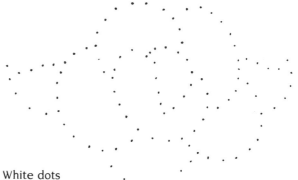

White dots

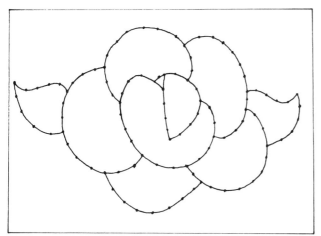

Diagram 9. Template

For the next step, position the rose template at the midpoint of one border. Secure to the quilt by using small pieces of masking tape on each corner. Next, dip a cotton puff into the baby powder, and shake off any excess. Using a circular motion, firmly rub the cotton over the entire template. If necessary, dip the cotton into the baby powder again, so that the entire template is covered. The circular motion will have forced the baby powder through the holes of the template. This next step is most important. **Very gently** remove the tape and then lift the template straight up and off the quilt without disturbing the powder. White dots of powder should remain on the quilt. Next, using the soapstone or soap, connect the dots to form a complete design (see Diagram 10).

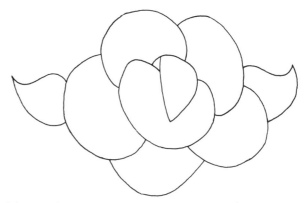

Diagram 10. Connect Dots to Form a Complete Design

It's important that the process described above be completed in an area free of drafts and that the quilt is spread flat and is secure so it won't shift in any way.

Using the above process, and proceeding around the border, continue to mark one rose at a time. Additional roses will be placed at the center of each border, as well as one on each corner. On the width of the quilt, six additional roses will be placed on each border, spaced evenly between the corners and the midpoint roses. On the length of the quilt, six additional roses will also be made on each border, again spaced evenly between the corners and the midpoint roses. Note that the twining is longer between the roses on the longer borders. This is illustrated next to the quilting design in the pattern section.

After all the roses have been marked on the quilt, the twining is drawn onto the borders. It was suggested earlier that the patterns for this be made separately. This is a good procedure because the lengths of the twinings can be adjusted to adapt to the differences in the distances between the roses. The length and width of the curves of the twining may be adjusted as desired. Simply use the templates as a guide and trace around the edges with the soapstone or sliver of soap. The sketch next to the pattern shows how the length of the twining has been adjusted from one side of the border to the other.

Quilting

After the layers are basted, it's time to start the quilting. This is the process in which the three layers are stitched together to form the completed quilt. In addition to holding the layers together, the quilting serves to give the quilt its texture. The surface of the quilt will recede or stand out depending on the amount and the design of the quilting. It is important to take as much care with the quilting as you did with the appliqué in order to have an attractive completed work.

The quilt shown was quilted with a variety of colors. Blue areas were quilted with blue thread, greens with green thread, reds with red thread, and so forth. In this particular design, using multiple colors was found to be more visually pleasing than using only one color throughout the quilt. A variety of colors also gives the back of the quilt an interesting visual effect. Use quilting thread to do the work. It is a stiffer thread and has a special coating that makes it stronger. With the wide variety of quilting threads available today, it's relatively easy to find enough colors to complete the design. If you have difficulty finding the threads, many quilting supply stores now stock threads other than those specifically labeled for quilting, and these will serve as acceptable substitutes. These other types of threads come in many colors and are strong enough to use for quilting, though running lengths through beeswax as you use them will give them added strength and durability.

The quilting can be done with the quilt in a frame, with the use of quilting hoops, or without either, depending on your individual preference. Proper basting will ensure that the three layers will not shift with any method that is chosen to complete the quilting process. With any method, the quilting should be started in the center of the quilt, with the work proceeding toward the edges. This will help ease any fullness out to the edges and will prevent wrinkles or excess puffiness from forming in the center of the quilt.

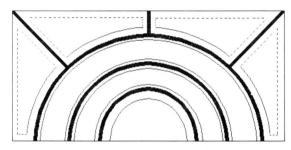

Diagram 11. Combination of Close and ¼" Stitching

On this quilt, the quilting has been done close to the black bias leading. This gives texture to the quilt, raising the glass away from the leading, yet the actual quilting is not highly visible on the front of the quilt. As an alternative, you can choose to echo quilt the leading by placing the quilting about ¼" (6 mm) away from it. The process for this was described earlier. Stitching in this way will give a somewhat different look to the quilt. Note that it will be difficult to maintain the ¼" (6 mm) margin throughout the quilt as some of the areas to be quilted are quite small. You can choose to quilt close to the leading in these areas and use the ¼" (6 mm) spacing only to accent certain of the larger areas. In this quilt, every glass piece was quilted with the outline quilting, although this is not necessary if you prefer less quilting (see Diagram 11). It's best to experiment and decide what you find most pleasing.

Remember also that you are not limited to just an outline quilting of the appliqué shapes. Experimenting with various quilting designs to fill in some of the spaces can add new interest and individuality to a quilt. As an example, the large expanse of the dove's body can be filled in with quilting to resemble feathers (see Diagram 12).

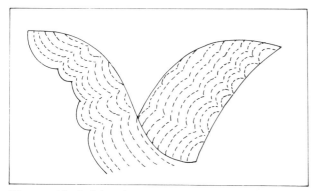

Diagram 12. Quilting the Dove's Wings

through top and batting at point where first stitch will be placed. Bring needle back up at opposite end of first stitch. Pull thread through until approximately 18" (46 cm) of the length is on each side of the first stitch. Take a small backstitch. The thread is now anchored. Proceed with the quilting. When the first length is used, you can then go back to the 18" (46 cm) tail. Thread the needle onto this and put the needle through the hole from which the thread is coming. Going only through the top and the batting, come up a stitch-length away from the beginning of the first quilting line. Take a small backstitch, and proceed to quilt in the opposite direction with this length of thread. Using this method, the thread is anchored without knots.

To begin the actual quilting, follow the steps as given below.

Step 1

Thread a needle with an appropriate color of thread and cut a length 18–20 inches (46–51 centimeters) long. If you've followed the suggested color scheme, use white thread, as you'll begin quilting with the dove in the center of the quilt. If you used another color scheme, begin with the color that you have chosen to make the dove.

Knot one end of the thread. Insert the needle through the top and batting only, a short distance (about ½" or 12 mm) from where the first stitch will actually be placed. Bring the needle up at the point of the first stitch. Pull length of thread through, and pop the knot through the top layer of the fabric. Pull until the tail of thread is also through the fabric. If the tail has been left too long, clip away excess. The knot is now buried in the batting. It's important that a knot does not show on the top or the bottom of a completed quilt. Take a small backstitch to anchor the thread, and then continue along the quilting line as instructed below, beginning with step 2.

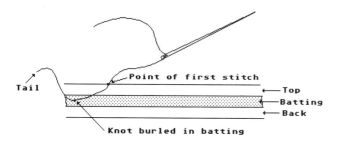

Alternative method

This method involves using a longer length of thread and no knots. It may be used only in an area where the quilting can proceed in both directions from where the first stitch is placed. Thread a needle and cut a length of thread 36–40 inches (98–102 centimeters) long. Do not tie a knot in either end. Insert the needle

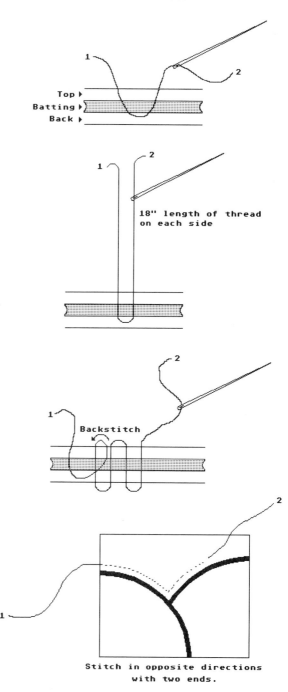

Stitch in opposite directions with two ends.

33

Step 2

Either a running or a stab stitch will be used to do the quilting. The method used will depend on which method you feel most comfortable with and can achieve the best results with in the finished quilting stitch. With either method, the completed stitch will look as shown, and will hold the three layers of the quilt together.

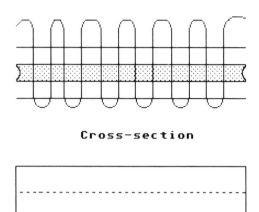

Cross-section

Top view

A **running stitch** consists of simply inserting the needle into the top layer at an angle, pushing it through all the layers, and with a rocking motion bringing it back up through all the layers to the top of the quilt. It can be done one stitch at a time, or several stitches may be taken on the needle before the thread is pulled through the layers.

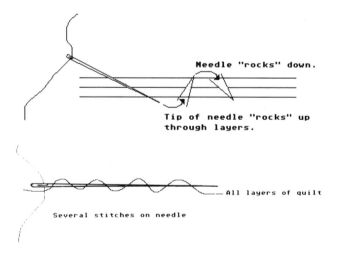

Needle "rocks" down.

Tip of needle "rocks" up through layers.

Several stitches on needle

All layers of quilt

It will take some practice to ensure that the stitches are the same length on the top and the bottom of the quilt. The best way to achieve this consistency with the running stitch is to develop a rocking motion. A rhythm develops between the hand on top of the quilt and the one below the quilt, with one pushing down and the other one pushing up. The needle is gently rocked in and out of the fabric. Many quilters use a single finger on the bottom, often the thumbnail, as a guide to judge the length of the stitch and to push the needle back up through the layers. Others find that using a thimble on the hand below the quilt is more helpful. It will take some trial and error to find the method you find most comfortable.

The **stab stitch** is preferred by some quilters. With this technique, the needle is "stabbed" straight down through all three layers. The hand beneath the quilt then pushes the needle straight back up at the beginning of the next stitch. Using this method, it will take some practice to ensure that the stitches on the back of the quilt are as straight as those on the front. At first, you may have difficulty judging where the quilting line is, and you may find that the stitches on the back are often zigzagged. This problem will decrease as you become more adept at the technique.

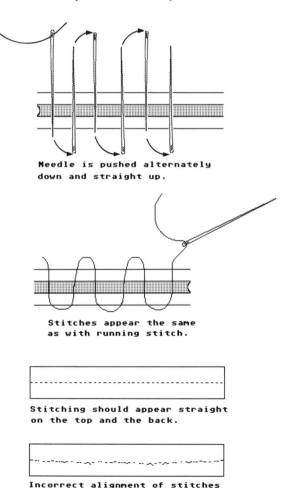

Needle is pushed alternately down and straight up.

Stitches appear the same as with running stitch.

Stitching should appear straight on the top and the back.

Incorrect alignment of stitches on back causes a zigzag effect.

Step 3

There are different methods used to end the stitching when the end of a thread is reached. As with many things in quilting, the method you choose depends on individual preference. Either method, when done properly, will securely anchor the thread.

The first method involves burying the thread in the batting without using a knot. Several inches of thread should be left at the end of the quilting for this to be done. At the final stitch, take a small backstitch and come back up to the top of the quilt. Now, put the needle back through the hole it just emerged from, but only go through the top and the batting. Pushing through the batting, bring the needle out through the top of the quilt again about 1" (2.54 cm) away. Pull the loop of thread through until it disappears through the quilt top. Again, put the needle back through the hole that it was just brought out of, but only go through the top and the batting. Pointing the needle in a different direction from the first time, go through the batting and bring the needle out on top again. Gently pull until loop of thread disappears.

Continue this process in a zigzag manner for a few more times. Clip the thread close to the top of the quilt on the last stitch, and allow the end of the thread to pop back into the batting. Weaving the thread through the batting in this manner will keep it secured without a knot.

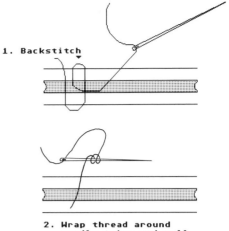

1. Backstitch

2. Wrap thread around needle twice and pull through to make a knot.

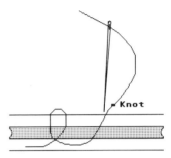

3. Put needle back through this hole and pull knot through behind it.

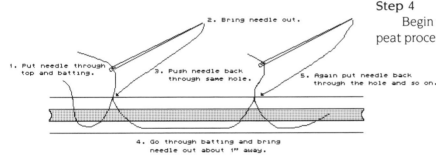

1. Put needle through top and batting.
2. Bring needle out.
3. Push needle back through same hole.
4. Go through batting and bring needle out about 1" away.
5. Again put needle back through the hole and so on.

The other method involves ending with a knot that is then popped through the top of the quilt into the batting. At the end of the stitching, take a small backstitch. As close to the top of the quilt as possible, wrap the thread around the needle two times and pull it through to form a knot. Hold the thread as close to the quilt as possible when doing this, just as when making a French knot in embroidery. Ideally, the knot should be no more than ¼" (6 mm) away from the quilt. Put the needle back through the hole formed at the end of the backstitch. Only go through the top layer and the batting. Bring needle up approximately 1" (2.54 cm) away. Pull the thread completely through, allowing the knot to pop through the top and into the batting. Clip the thread and let the end slip back into the batting.

Step 4

Begin with a new thread and continue quilting. Repeat process until all of the area in the hoop or frame is quilted.

Step 5

Move frame or hoop to a new section of the quilt. Quilt this area.

Step 6

Continue quilting, moving to new sections of the quilt until all of the quilting is complete. Remember to always work from the center to the edges. Take care not to wrinkle the fabric or catch any extra fullness in the frame or the hoop when beginning a new section of the quilt. Some quilters find that holding the edge of the quilt is easier than using a hoop once the final border is reached. Others pin a piece of cloth to the edge, which can then be put in the hoop. This leaves the edge of the quilt free to stitch. If enough excess is left on the backing, it will serve the same purpose.

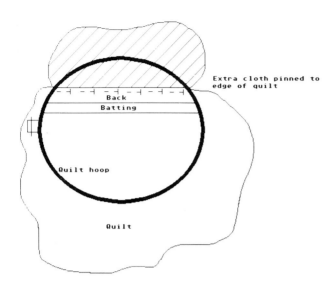

Extra cloth pinned to
edge of quilt

Back

Batting

Quilt hoop

Quilt

Step 7

When all of the quilting is complete, remove any remaining basting that may not have been removed as the quilting was being done. Then trim the excess batting and back at this time. Trimming these edges slightly wider than the top will allow enough fabric to ensure that the binding is consistently full all around the quilt, with no thin areas. Now it's time to proceed to binding the quilt.

Binding the Quilt

To make bias binding, follow instructions for continuous bias binding that are found earlier in the text. It will require about 10–11 yards (9–10 meters) of ¼" (6 mm) finished, double-thickness binding to go around the quilt. Once the bias has been cut, folded in half, and pressed, it is ready to be applied to the quilt. Bias will first be machine-stitched to the back of the quilt. Then it will be turned over the edge of the quilt and hand-stitched to the front. In this way, no machine stitching will show on the front of the quilt.

Step 1

Pin the bias to the back edge of the quilt, starting in the center of one side and continuing to within ¼" (6 mm) of the corner. Match the edges of the bias to the edge of the quilt top. This means that the bias will be back from the edge of the backing, if the backing has been cut wider than the top.

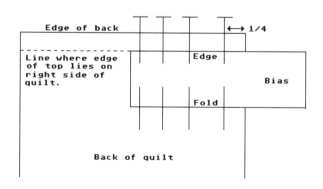

Step 2

The corners of the bias will be mitered as the bias is applied. Using ¼" (6 mm) seam, and leaving the first 4" (10 cm) of the bias loose, sew bias to within ¼" (6 mm) of the corner. End stitching.

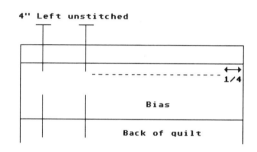

Step 3

Beginning at the point of the corner of the quilt, fold bias back on a 45-degree angle. Then fold bias forward along the edge of the quilt as was done on the first side. Pin.

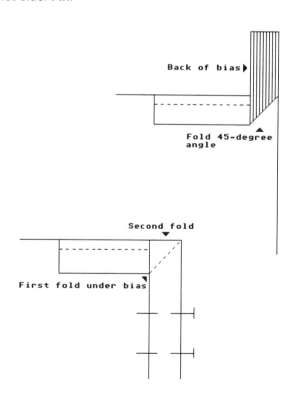

Step 4

Continue stitching second side of quilt, beginning ¼" (6 mm) from the corner. Take care not to catch the fold of fabric.

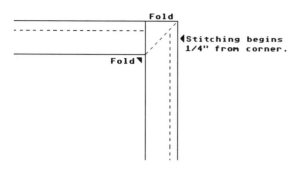

Step 5

Continue pinning and stitching around the quilt, treating each corner the same. The miters will be completed when the hand-stitching is done on the front of the quilt.

Step 6

When on the last side of the quilt, stitch the bias until within about 4" (10 cm) of the beginning end of the bias. Pin from the end of the stitching to where the two ends of the bias meet. Clip bias, leaving a tail about 3" (7.6 cm) long, extending beyond this meeting.

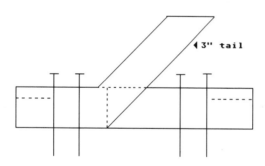

Unpin first end of bias. At about the midpoint of this loose end, unfold the bias. Now fold this open end of the bias back on itself at a 45-degree angle. Press fold.

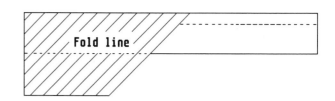

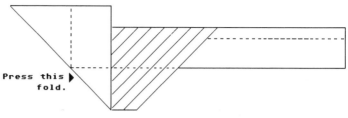

Pin adjoining end of bias along edge of quilt to the point where it meets the first bias. Repeat the process of folding with this end of the bias, but this folded bias end will point down instead of up. Press.

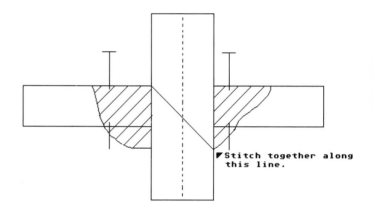

At this point, the bias flaps may be rather long. This is because extra has been allowed to provide for ease when working with the ends. Unpin the ends of the bias again. The fold lines that have been pressed into the fabric show where the seam line will be. With right sides together, stitch the two ends of the bias together along these pressed lines. Trim the ends of the bias off, leaving a ¼" (6 mm) seam. Again fold the bias in half, and pin it to the quilt. Stitch the space between the previous stitchings.

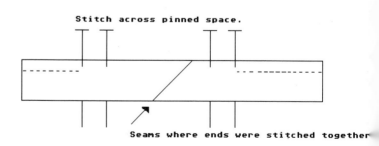

The machine-stitching of the bias is now complete. The remaining steps in applying the bias will be done by hand.

Step 7

Beginning on one side, turn the bias over to the front edge of the quilt and blind-stitch in place. Stitch along the side until almost reaching the corner.

Step 8

To complete the miter of the corner, hand-stitch to within ¼" (6 mm) of the corner.

Next, begin to fold over the bias on the next side of the quilt. Take care to ensure that a perfect miter is made along the dotted line as shown in Figure A, below.

A completed miter will look as shown in Figure B. The mitered corner will have the same appearance on the front and the back of the quilt. A few blind stitches will hold the miter in place. After completing the miter, continue hand-stitching around the quilt until all of the bias is turned and stitched. Treat each of the remaining three corners the same as the first corner.

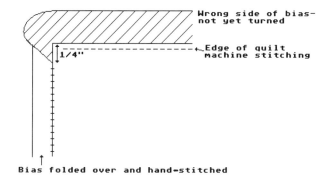

Wrong side of bias—
not yet turned

Edge of quilt
machine stitching

1/4"

Bias folded over and hand-stitched

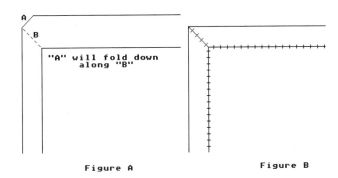

A

B

"A" will fold down
along "B"

Figure A

Figure B

Signing the Quilt

The final step in making a quilt is your signature. This step is important for several reasons. First, you've devoted many hours to the project. It is something that you can be proud of accomplishing. As with any work of art, a signature lets those viewing the quilt know the name of the artist.

Second, it will be important for those possessing the quilt in years to come to know the history of it: Who made it, where it was made, and other pertinent information will add interest to the quilt and will help bring the art and its artist to life for those enjoying it in years to come.

Third, the name on the quilt helps identify ownership in shows and/or for insurance purposes.

Individual quilters choose different ways to sign their quilts. Many choose to simply embroider the information on the back of the quilt, usually in one of the corners. This information should include a minimum of the quilter's name, the year the quilt was made, the state in which it was made, and the name of the quilt pattern.

Back of quilt

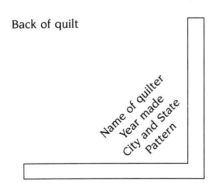

Others choose to incorporate their signature into the quilting design. This can be done at almost any point, depending on how it can be worked into the design. This marking, like the other, should include the name of the quilter, the state, and the year made. One disadvantage to this method is that it is often difficult for others to pick the information out of the other quilting.

Many quilters are now choosing to have their signatures quite visible from the front of the quilt, just as other artists sign a painting. This is often done with embroidery, and the position of the signature should be based on where it can best enhance the design rather than create a distraction. For example, on the Window of Peace quilt, the signature could be embroidered onto one of the black borders in a very dark gray thread. This way, the signature would show without providing too stark a contrast.

Whichever method you choose, certain information should always be kept with a quilt. I like to type this information on a piece of muslin which can then be easily tacked to the back of the quilt. Any information you feel is important is then kept with the quilt. All kinds of significant information about the quilt can be passed on in this way. It may include your name, when the quilt was made, where it was made, for whom it was made and that person's relationship to the quilter, any awards won, the name of the design, significance of the fabrics used, number of hours to make, if it's an original design, if it was the quilter's first quilt, and so forth (see Diagram 13).

Name of quiltmaker: _____

City: _____ State: _____

Year quilt made: _____ Made for: _____

Relationship to quilter: _____

Name of design: _____

Copyright notice (if applicable): _____

Any pertinent information: _____

_____

_____

_____

_____

_____

_____

_____

_____

_____

Diagram 13. Example of a Label for the Back of a Quilt

Patterns

Dove and Rainbow Pattern

Due to the size limitations of the text, it was necessary to divide the pattern for the rainbow and dove center medallion into 12 equal sections. These sections are put together as illustrated below to form a complete pattern. Starting from the top, sections A, B, C, D, E, and F will be joined together to form the left side of the medallion. Again starting from the top, sections G, H, I, J, K, and L will be joined to form the right side of the piece. Joining the left and the right sides will give the complete pattern. A single section of the design will be found on each of the pages that follow. Each section is clearly marked. The sections may be put together by matching the broken lines.

Note: To help keep track of the top and bottom of a section, pay attention to the solid lines. On section A, for example, the solid line will be found at the top and to the left. On sections B, C, D, and E, the solid line is found only on the left. Section F has a solid line to the left and on the bottom. The solid lines will be found to the opposite side on the sections for the right side of the medallion.

Color	No.	Color	No.
Very pale blue	1	Khaki green	31
Pale blue	2	Light violet	32
Medium sky-blue	3	Medium violet	33
Medium blue	4	Medium lilac	34
French blue	5	Medium grape	35
Cornflower blue	6	Medium purple	36
Periwinkle blue	7	Dark purple	37
Dark blue	8	Pale pink	38
Midnight blue	9	Light pink	39
Navy blue	10	Medium pink	40
Teal-blue	11	Dark raspberry	41
Turquoise	12	Carnation pink	42
Blue-gray	13	Hot pink	43
Pale Yellow	14	Dusty rose	44
Light lemon-yellow	15	Medium rose	45
Light yellow	16	Light red	46
Medium Yellow	17	Medium red	47
Goldenrod	18	Deep red	48
Yellow-orange	19	Medium maroon	49
Yellow-gold	20	Dark maroon	50
Orange-gold	21	Dark tan	51
Gold	22	Sepia	52
Spring green	23	Dark brown	53
Kelly green	24	Pale apricot	54
Green	25	Palest peach	55
Dark green	26	Cream	56
Dark pine-green	27	Gray	57
Forest green	28	Purplish-gray	58
Apple green	29	White	59
Olive	30		

A	G
B	H
C	I
D	J
E	K
F	L

Large Rose

Iris

44

Bleeding Heart

Tulip

Columbine

Daffodil

Fire Lily

Gentian

Morning Glory

Orchid

48

Pansy

Poppy

Saffron

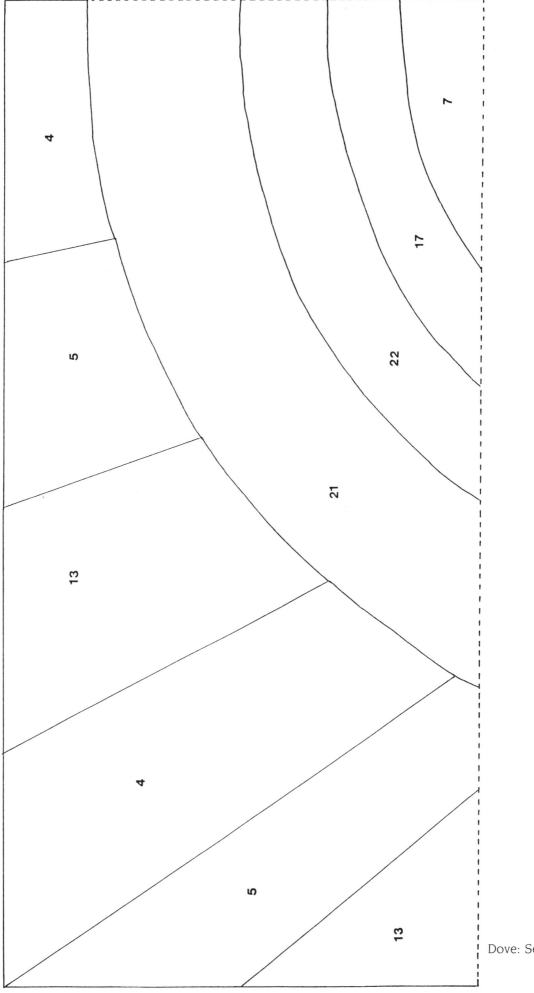

Dove: Section A

51

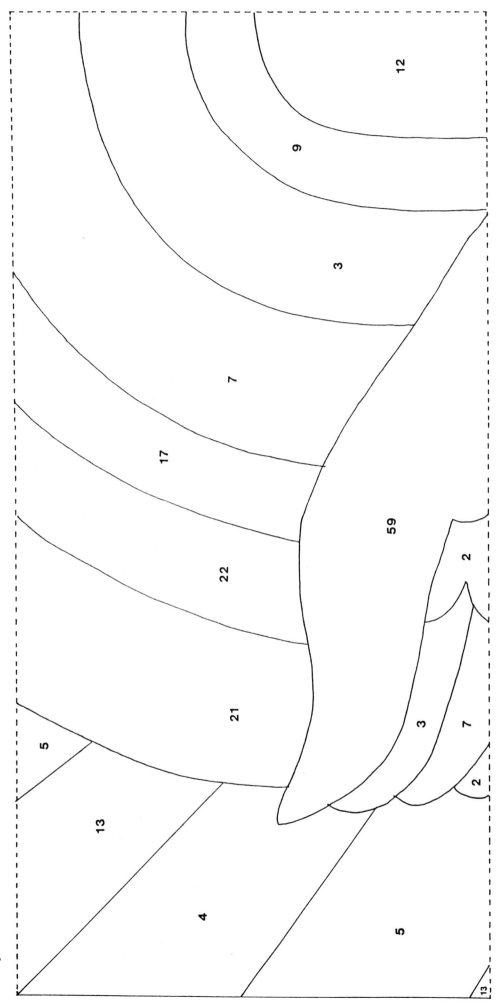

Dove: Section B

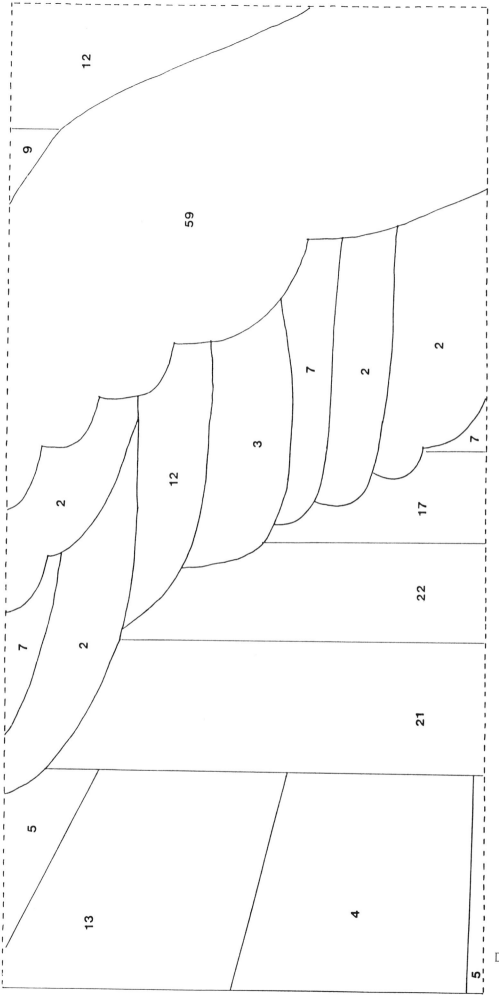

Dove: Section C

53

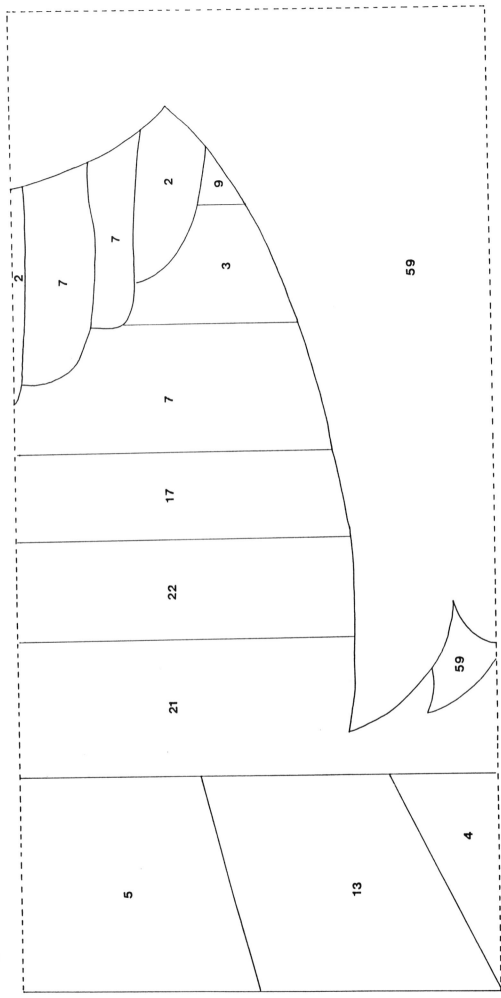

Dove: Section D

54

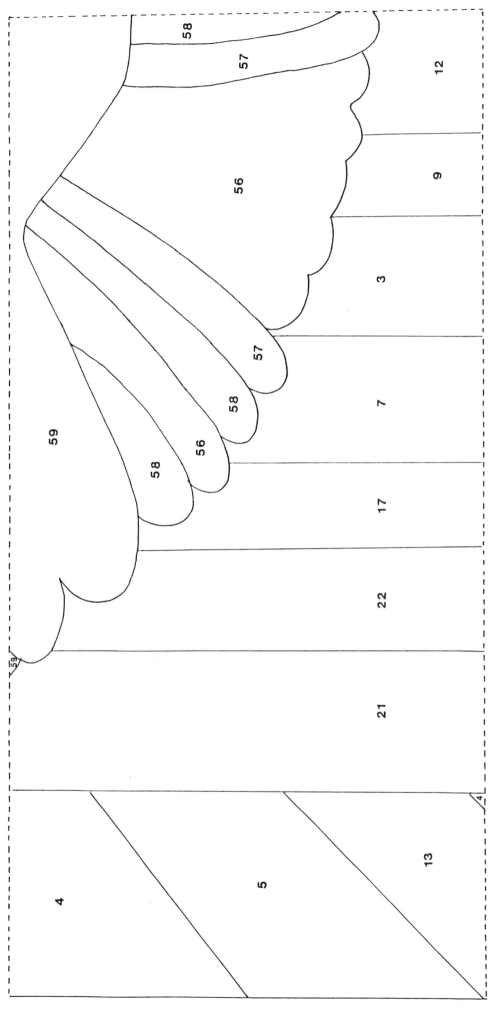

Dove: Section E

55

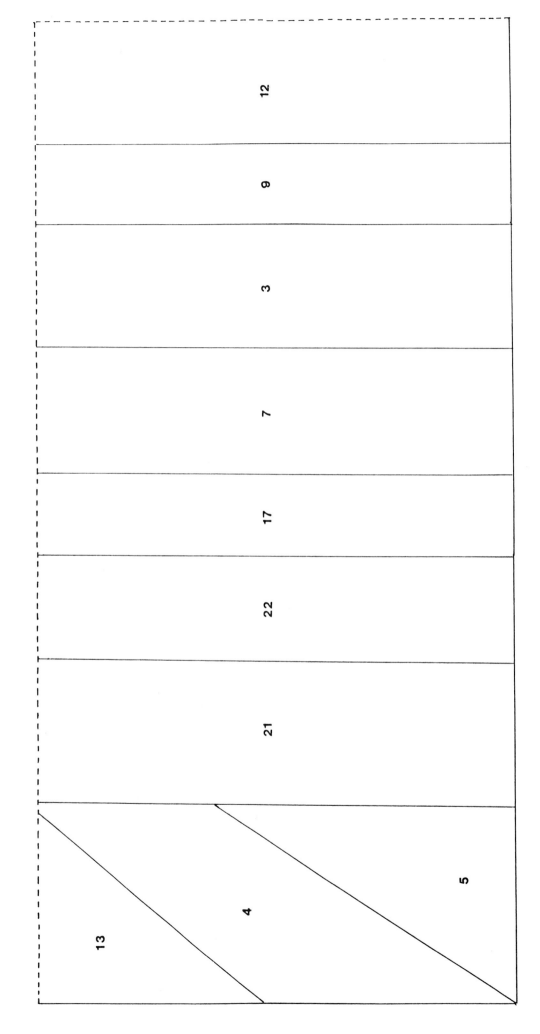

Dove: Section F

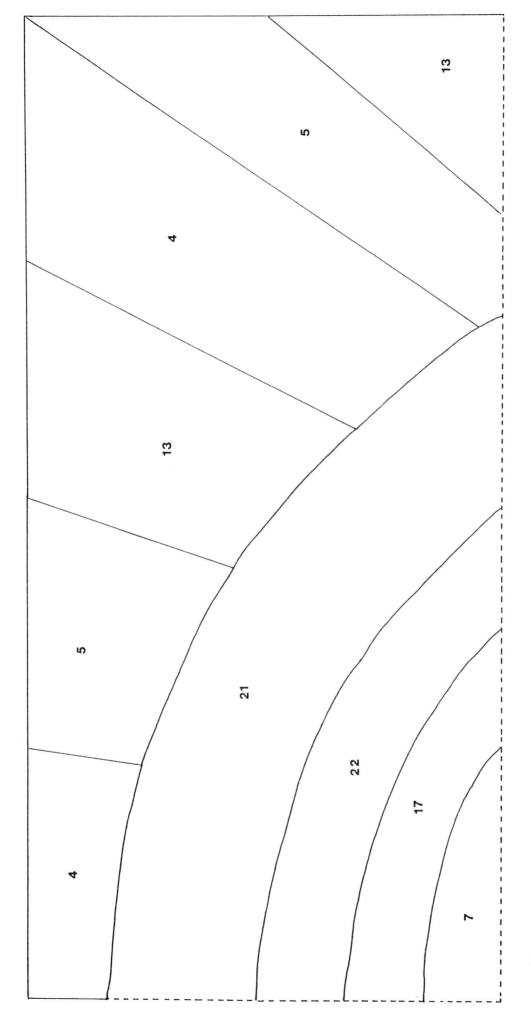

Dove: Section G

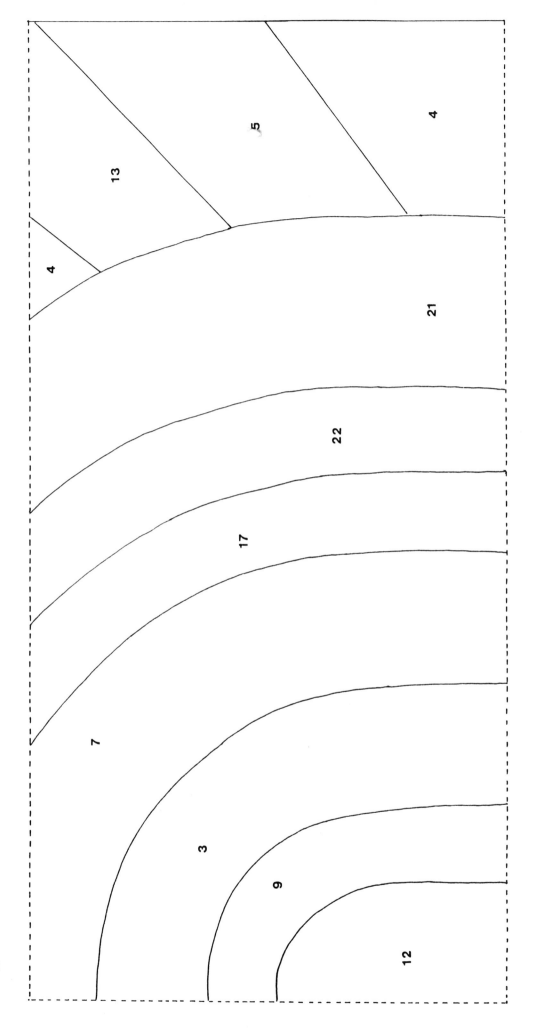

Dove: Section H

58

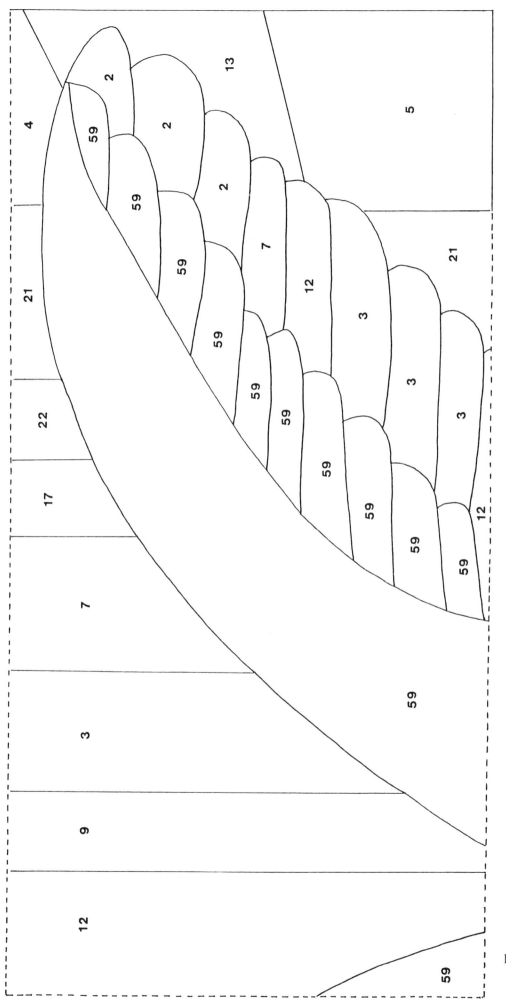

Dove: Section I

59

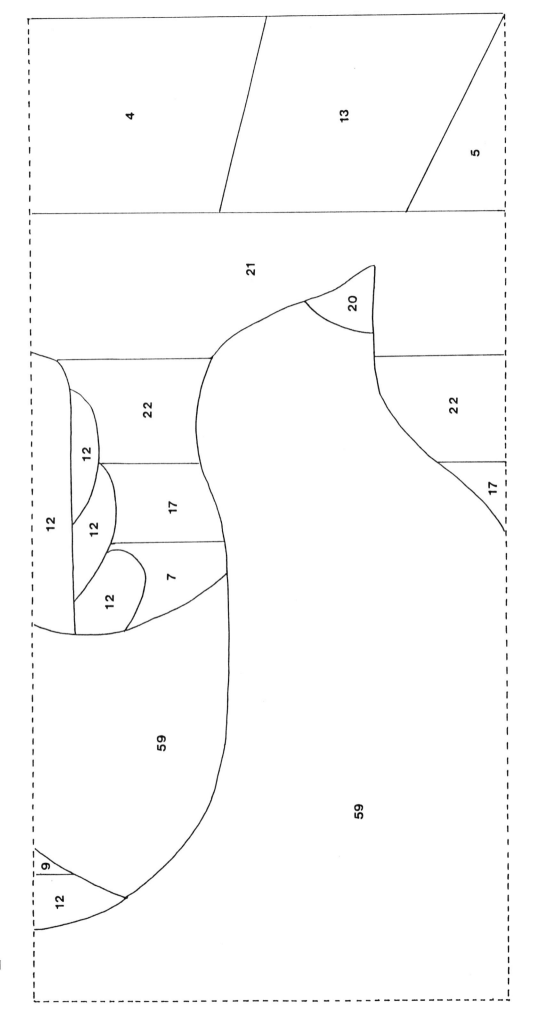

Dove: Section J

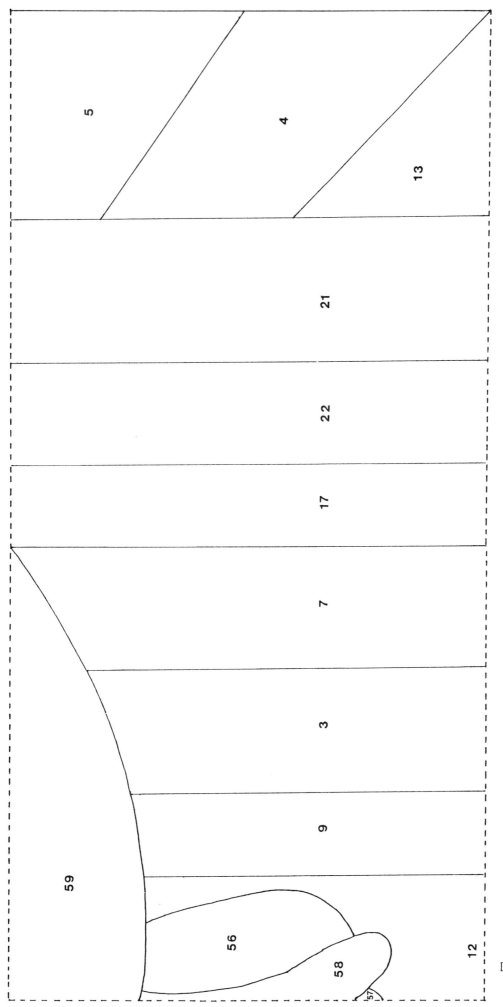

Dove: Section K

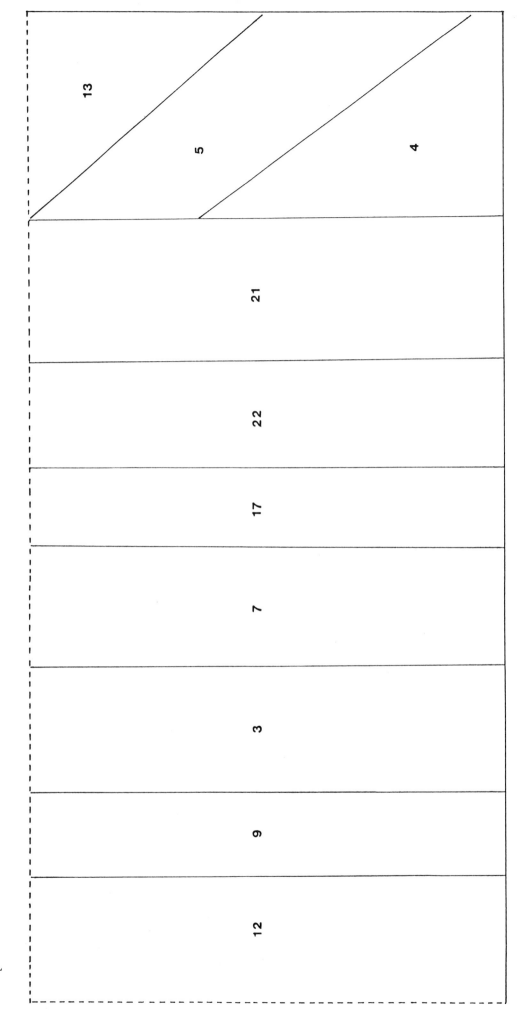

Dove: Section L

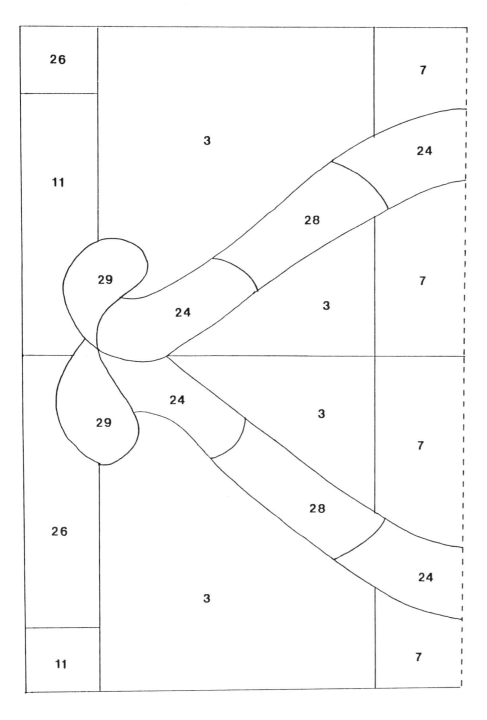

The pattern for the rose border is given in eight sections. As shown, different sections will need to be combined in order to make the two varied lengths of the border. The horizontal borders above and below the dove, the rose border, will require sections 3, 4, 5, and 6. The vertical borders on each side of the dove, the extended rose border, will require sections 1, 2, 4, 5, 7, and 8.

Border: Section 1

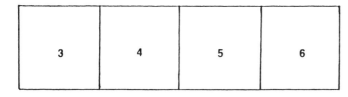

Rose border: Uses sections 3, 4, 5, and 6.

1	2	4	5	7	8

Extended rose border: Uses sections 1, 2, 4, 5, 7, and 8.

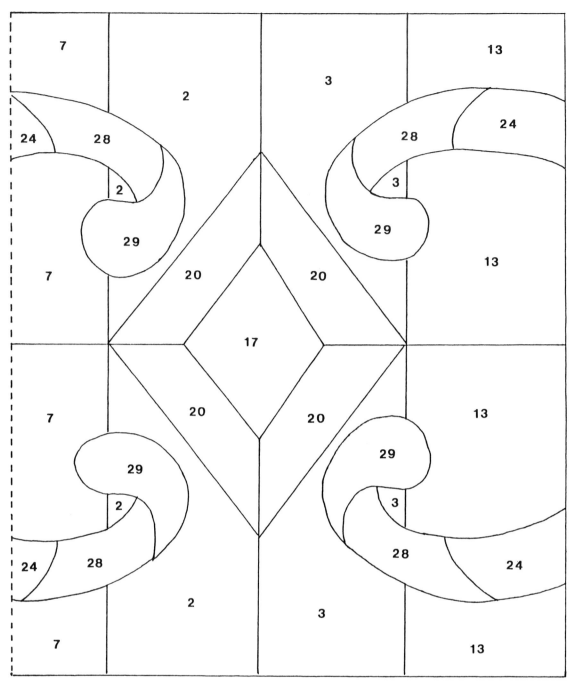

Border: Section 2

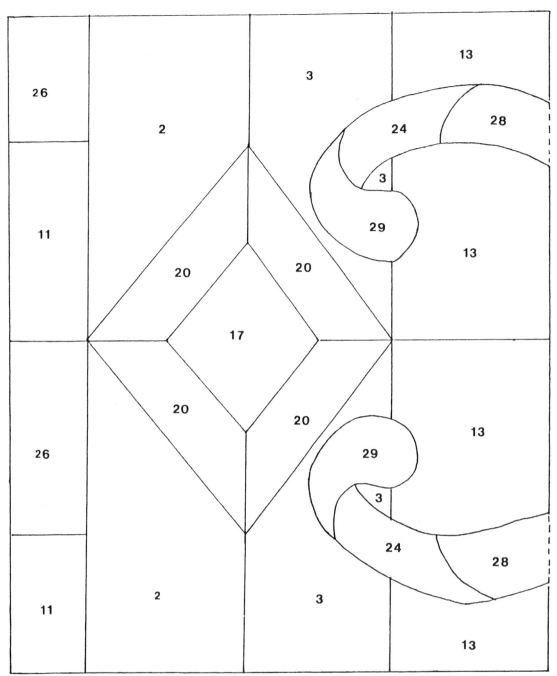

Border: Section 3

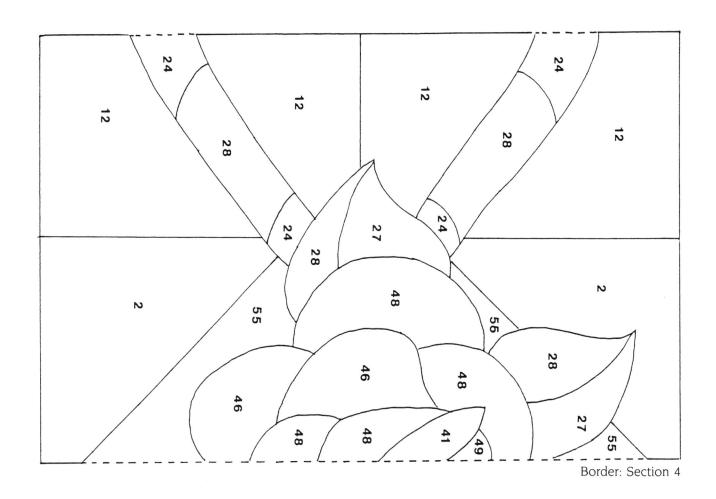

Border: Section 4

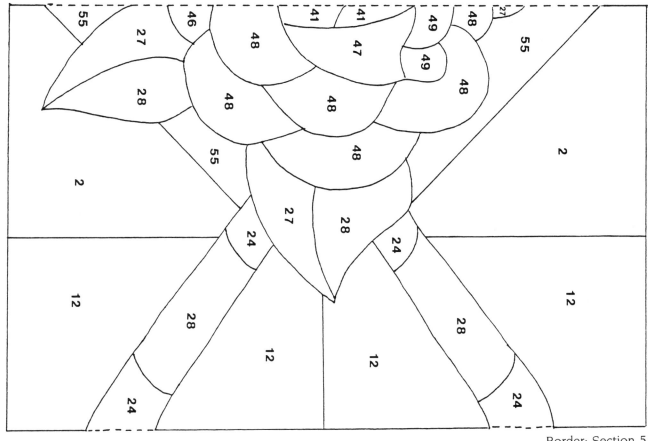

Border: Section 5

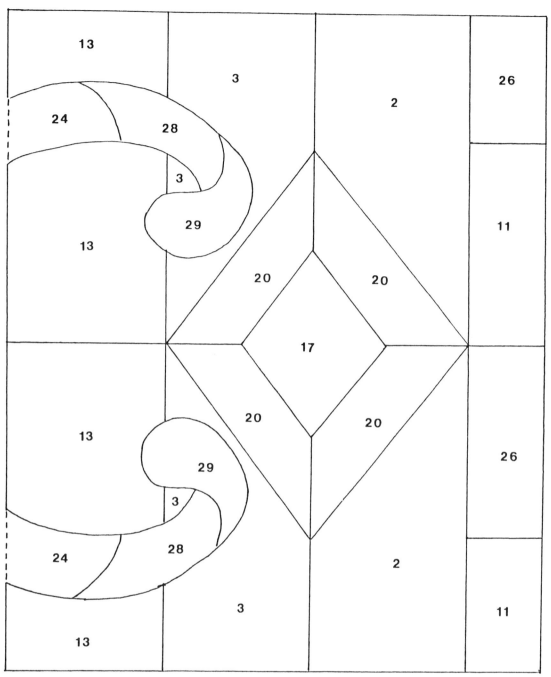

Border: Section 6

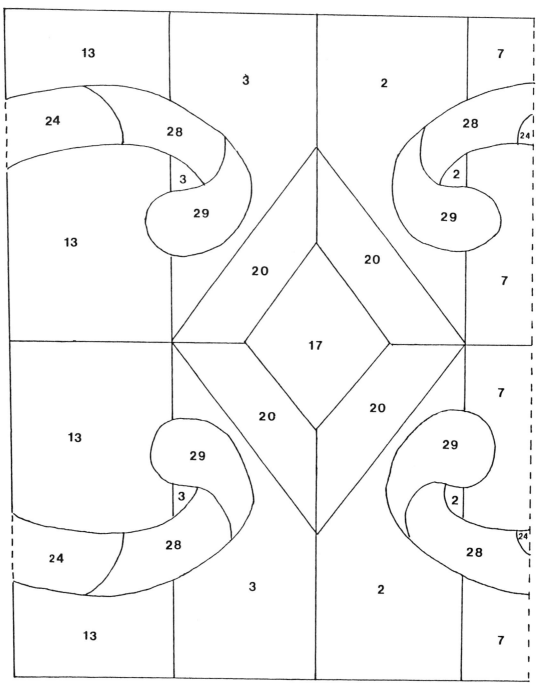

Border: Section 7

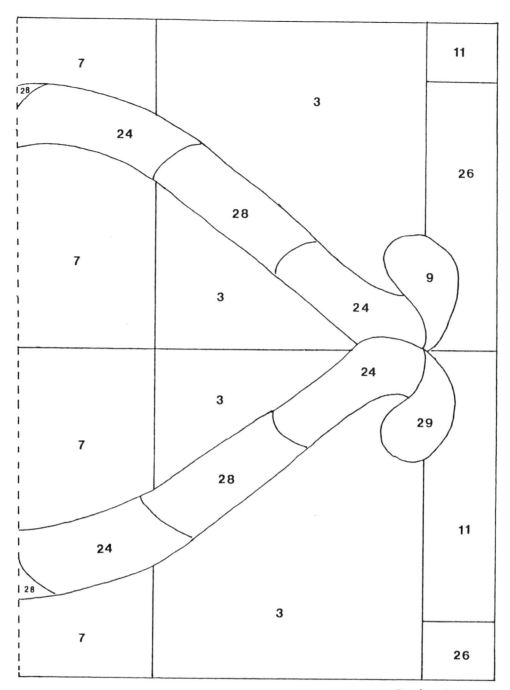

Border: Section 8

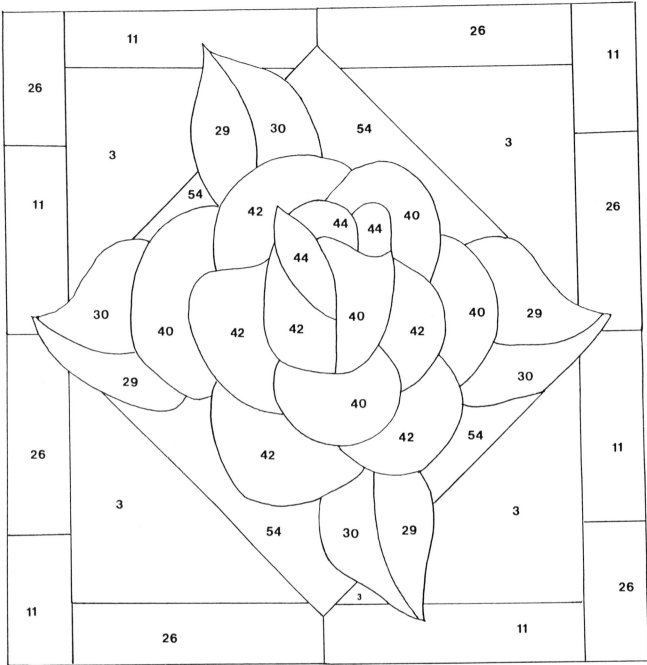

Small Rose

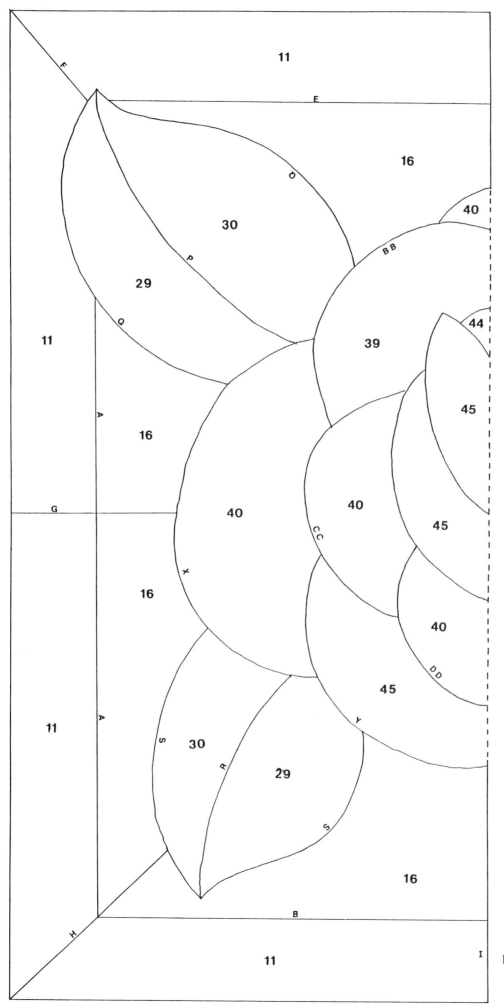

Large Rose

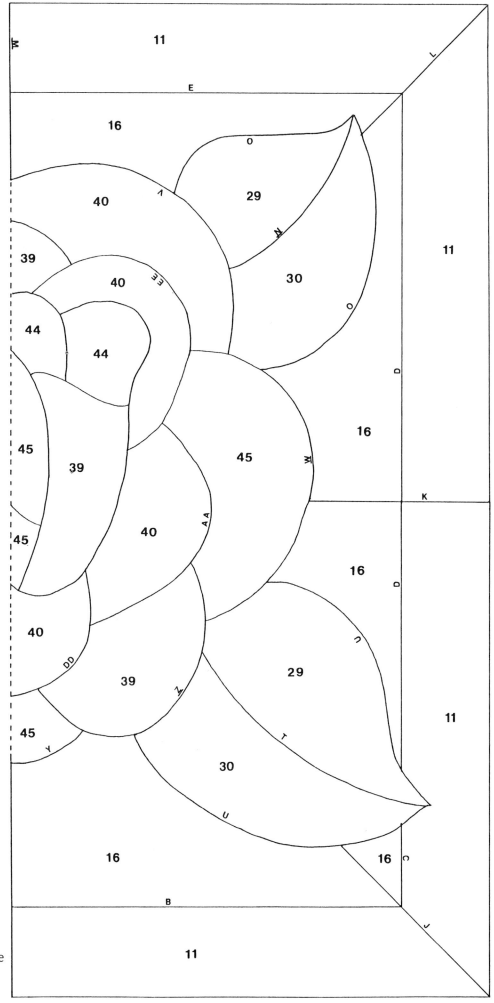

Large Rose

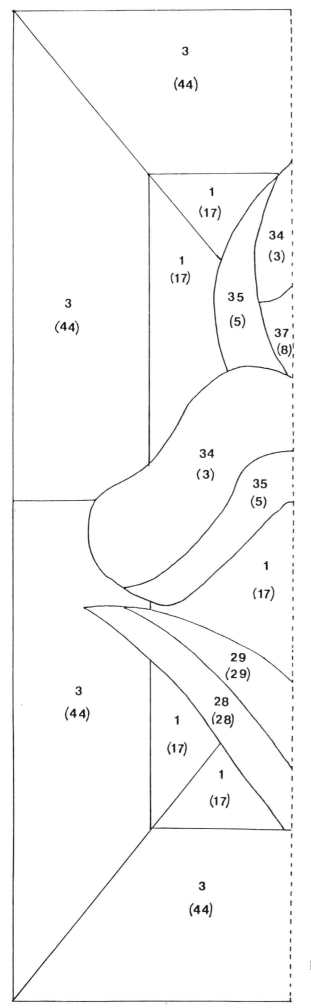

3

(44)

1

(17)

1

(17)

34

(3)

35

(5)

37

(8)

3

(44)

34

(3)

35

(5)

1

(17)

29

(29)

3

(44)

28

(28)

1

(17)

1

(17)

3

(44)

Iris

Note: Two sets of numbers are given on the pattern for the iris. The first set identifies the colors that will be needed for two of the iris blocks found in the quilt. The second set of numbers, which is found in parentheses, identifies the colors that will be needed for the two reverse iris blocks.

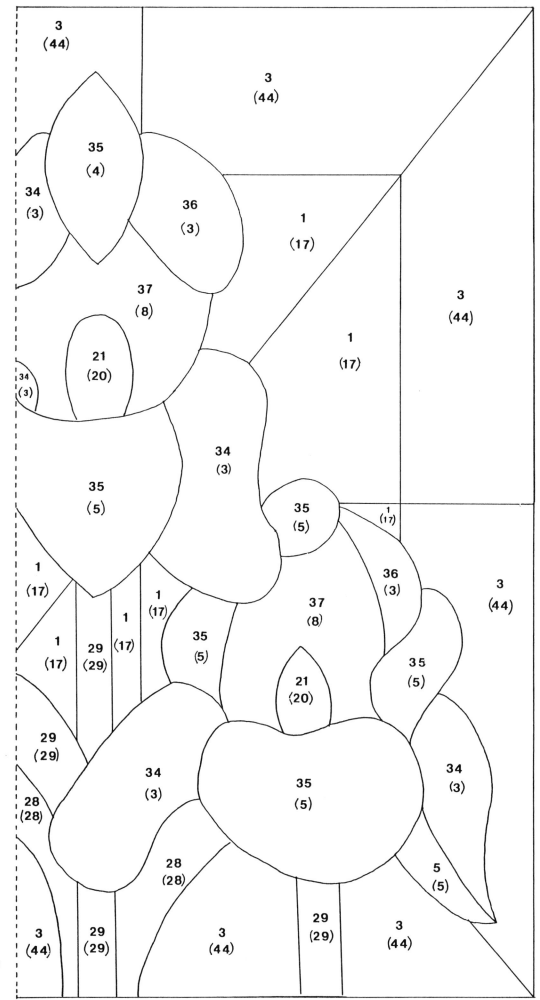

Iris

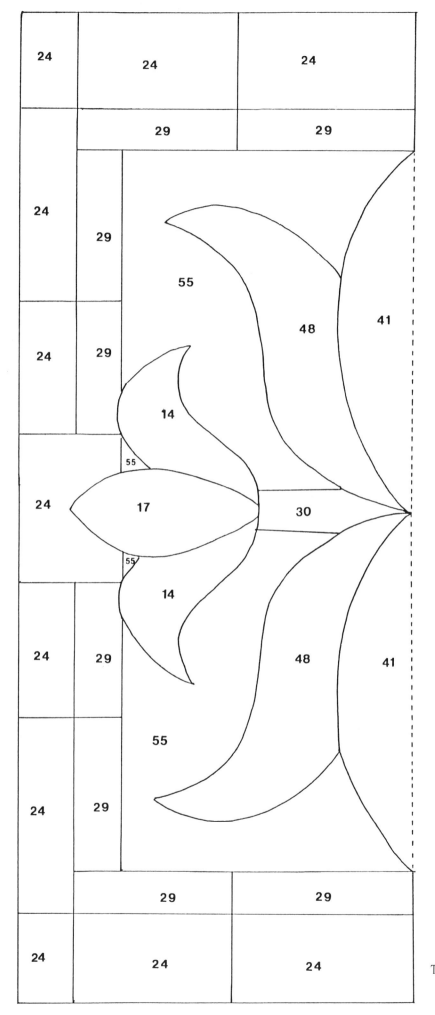

Tulip

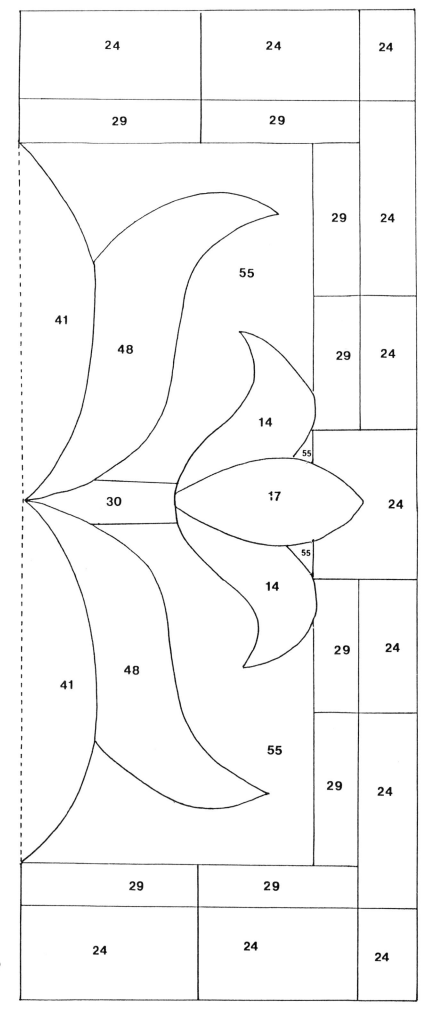

Tulip

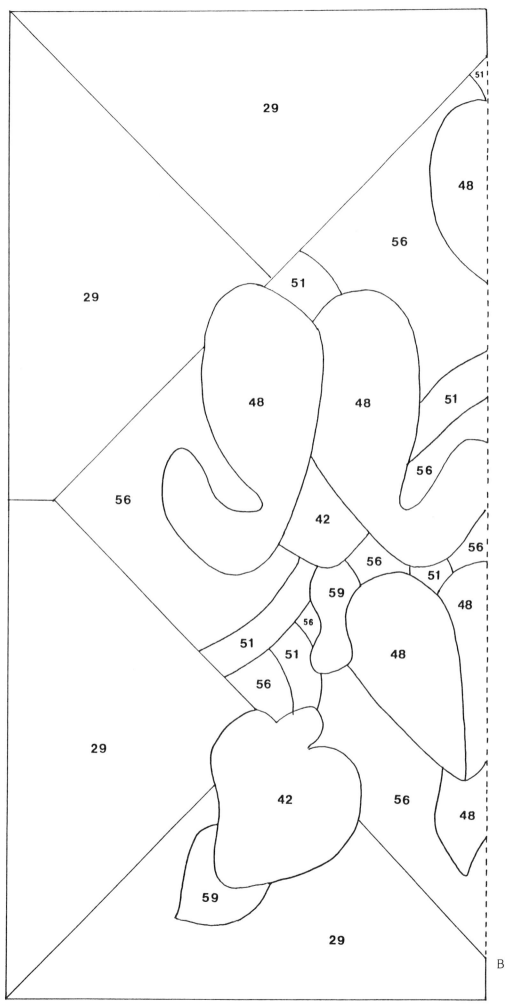

Bleeding Heart

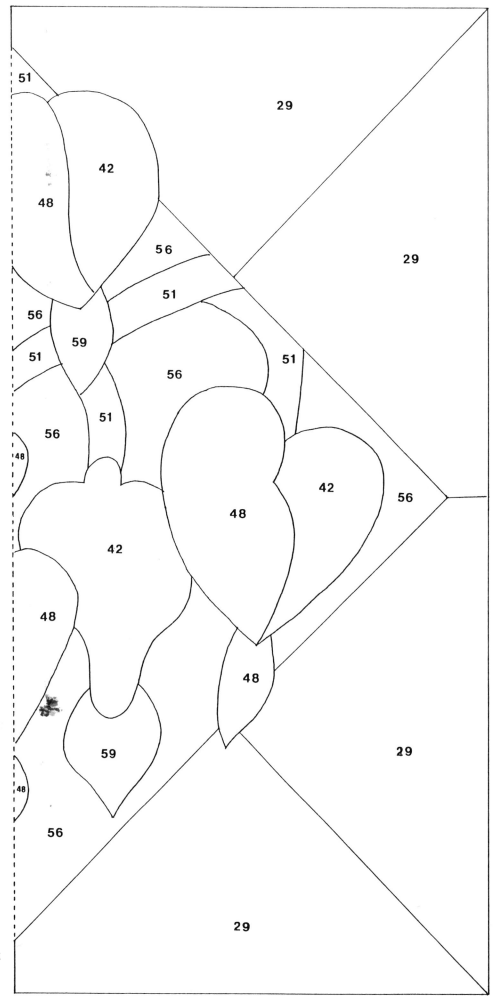

Bleeding Heart

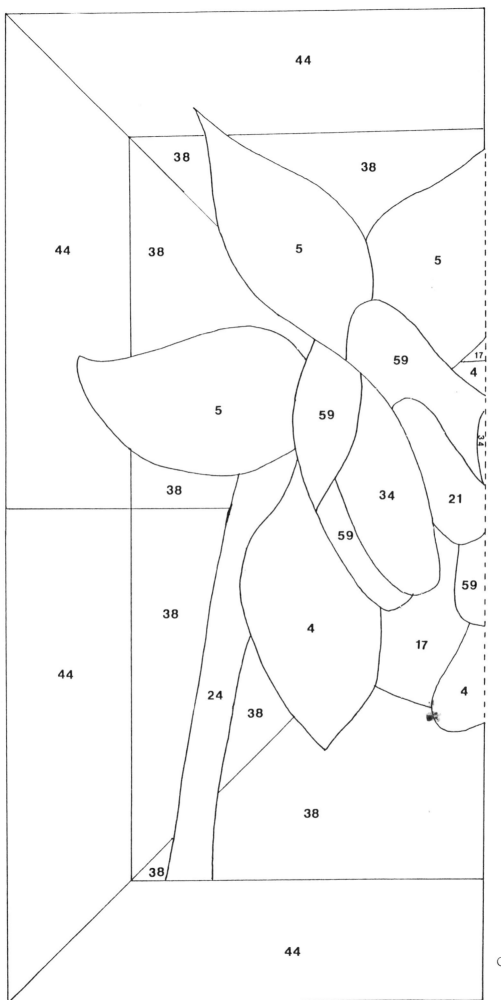

Columbine

79

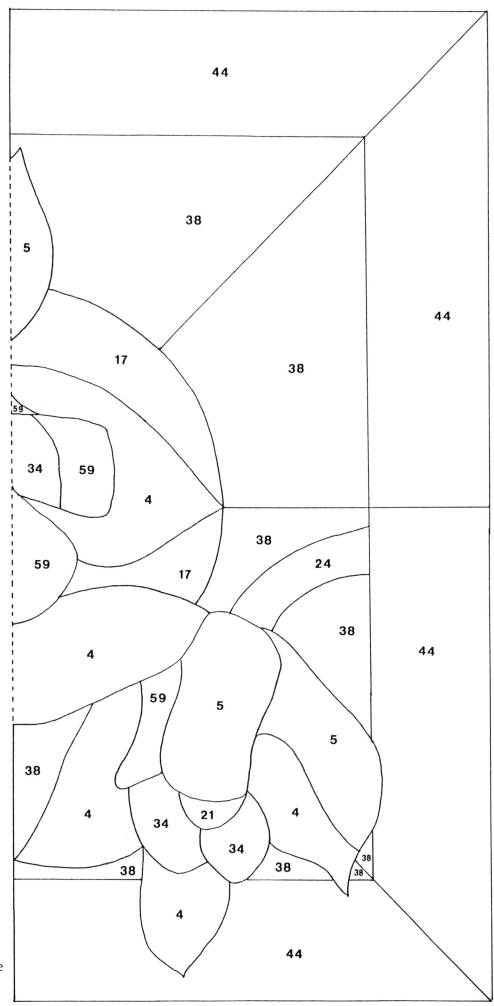

Columbine

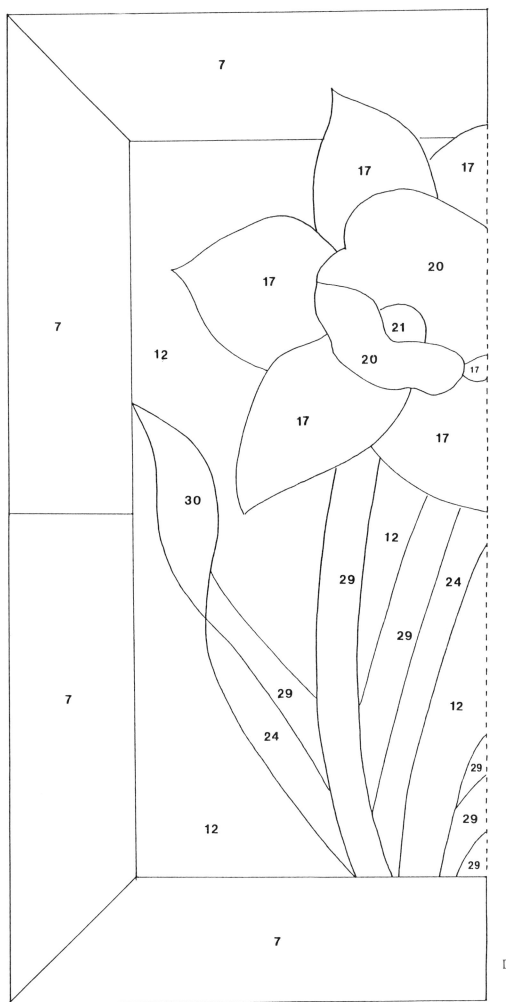

Daffodil

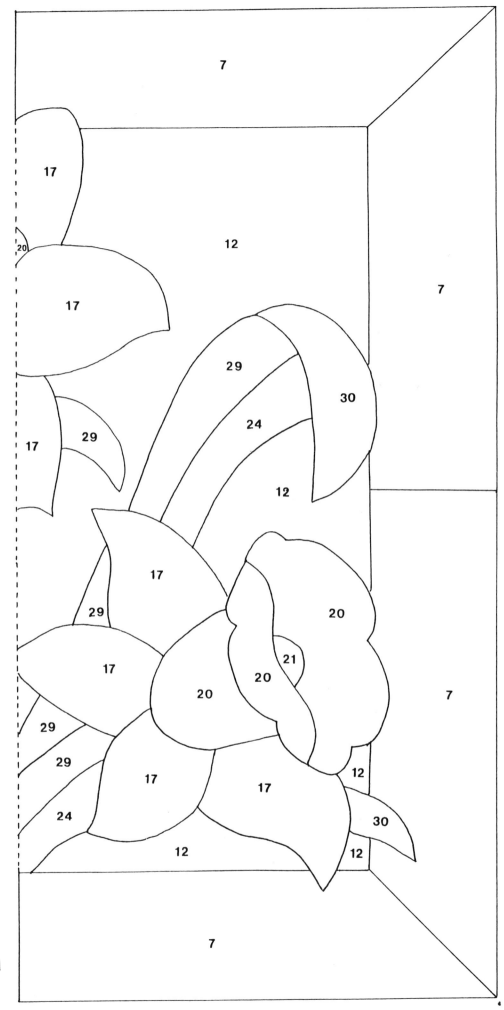

Daffodil

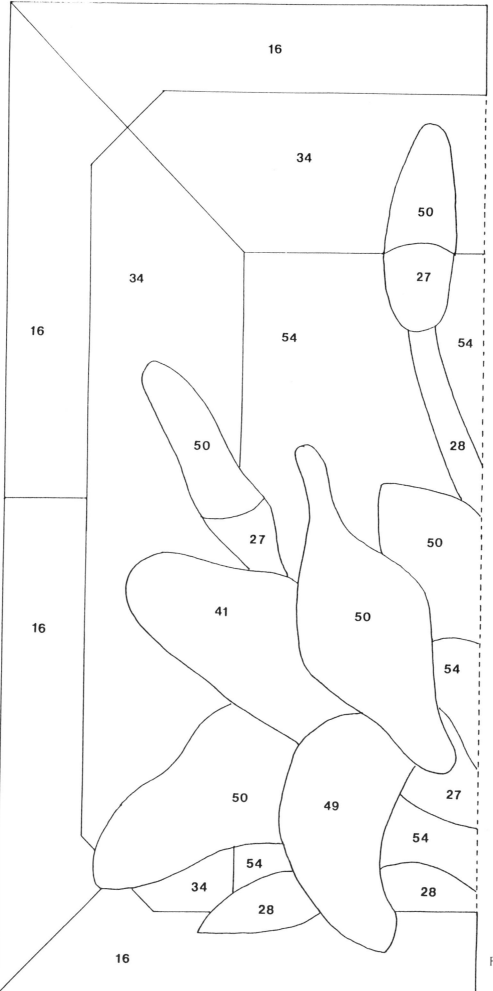

Fire Lily

83

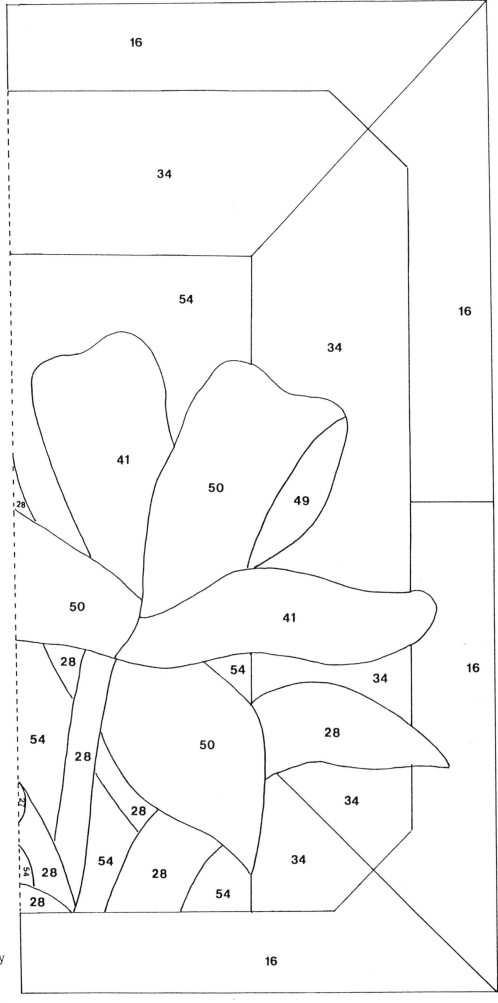

Fire Lily

84

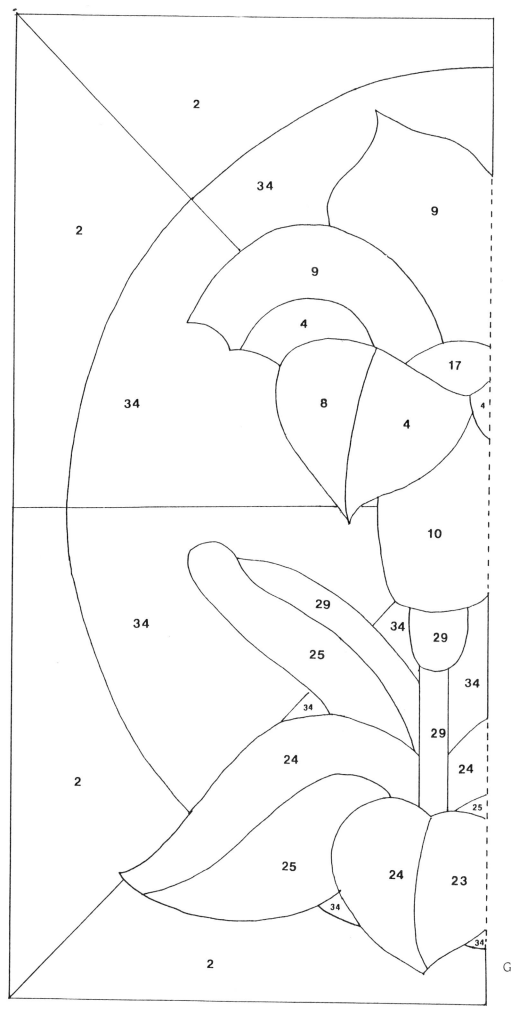

Gentian

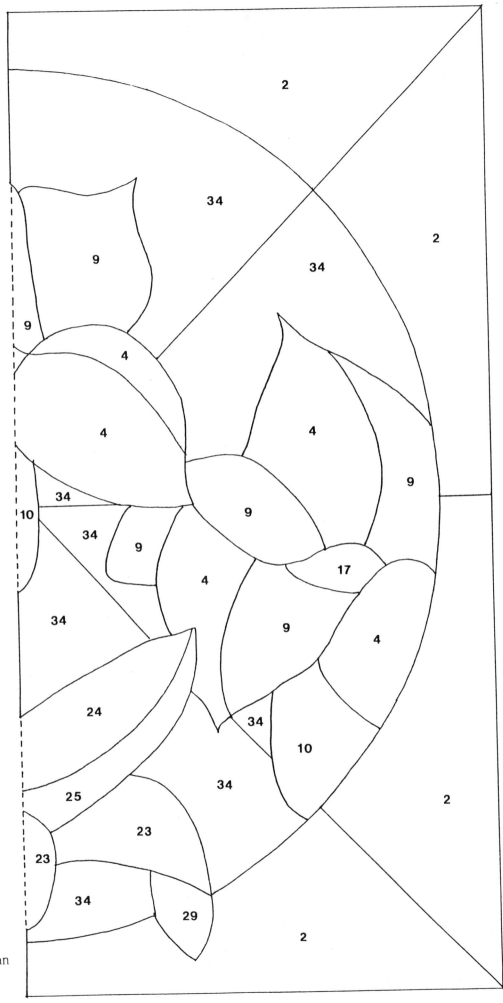

Gentian

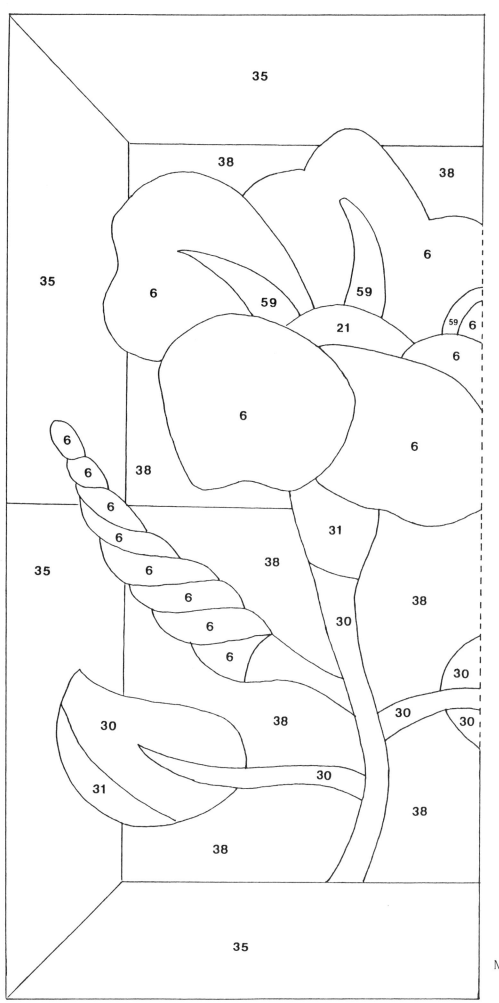

Morning Glory

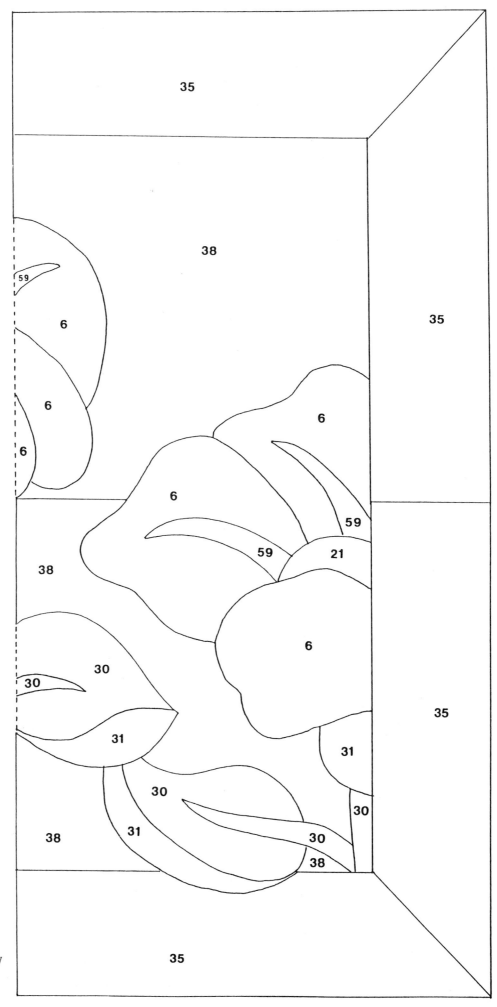

Morning Glory

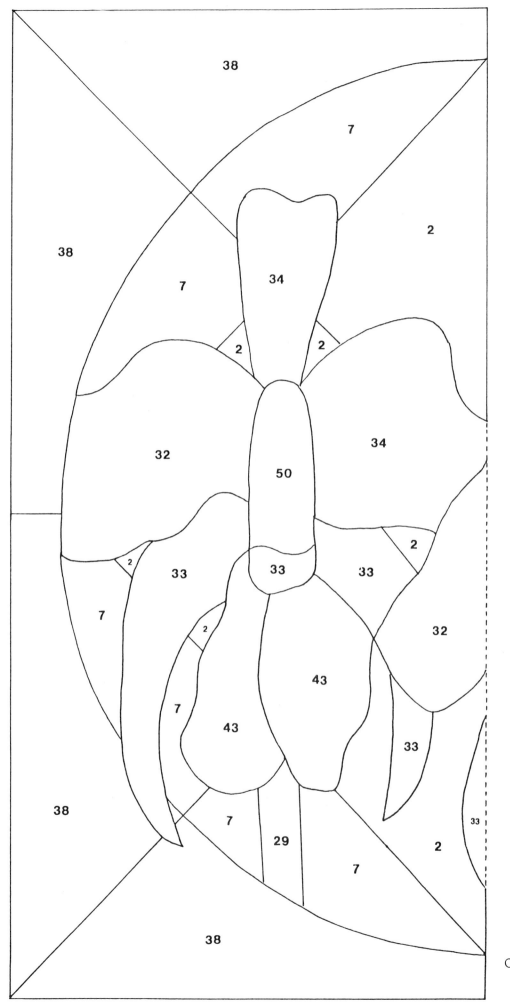

Orchid

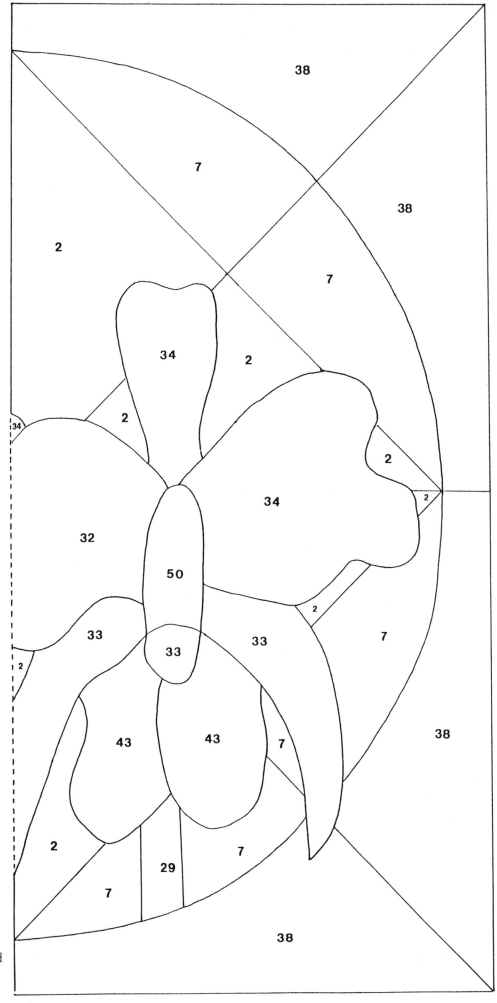

Orchid

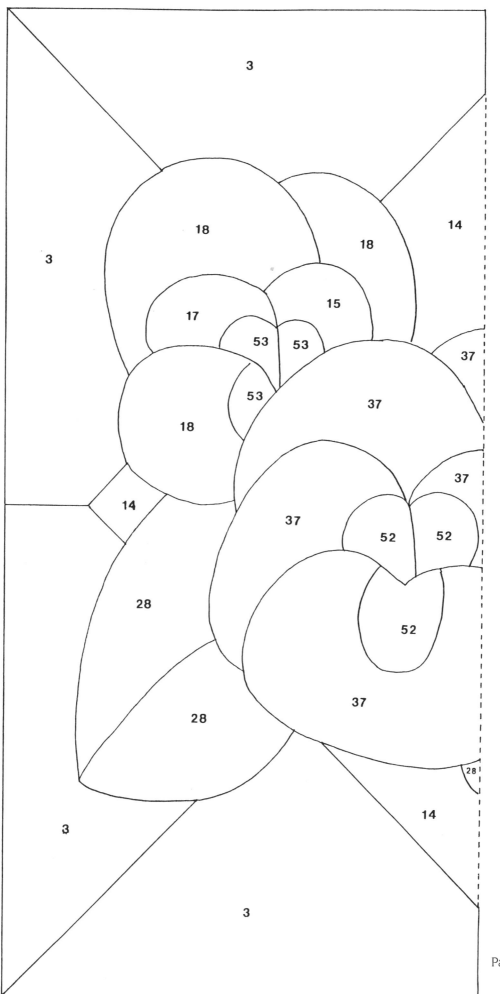

Pansy

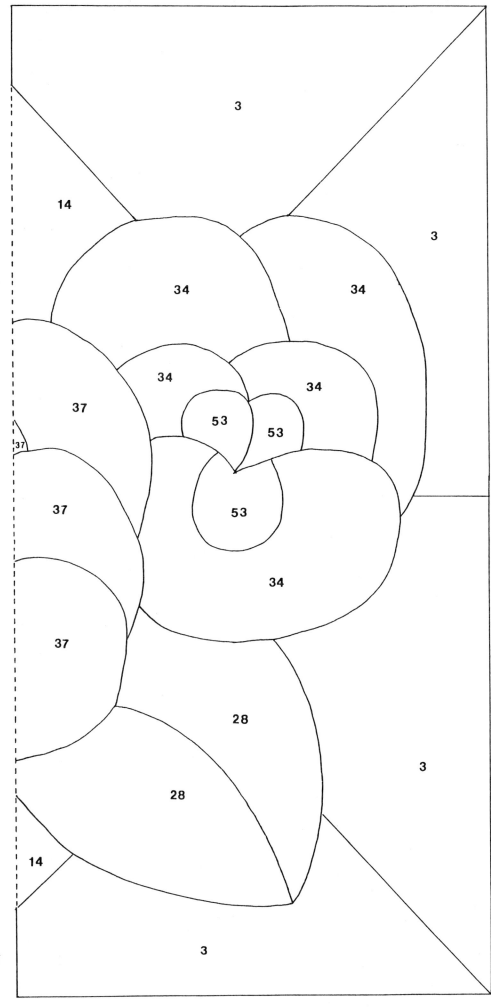

Pansy

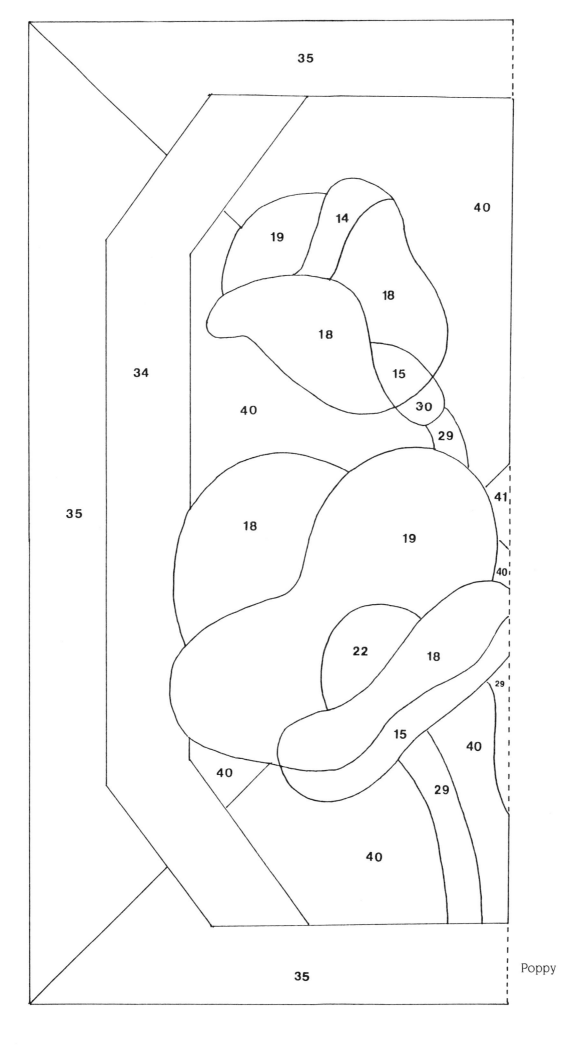

Poppy

93

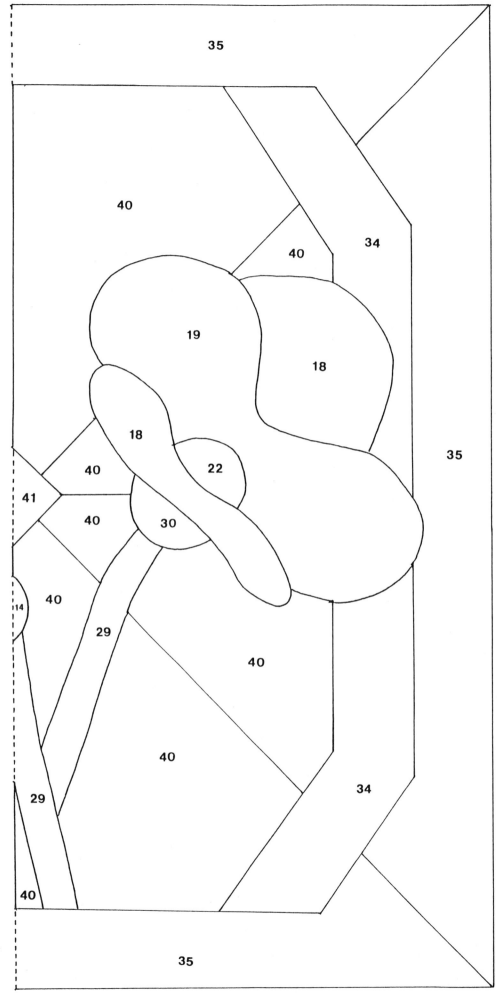

Poppy

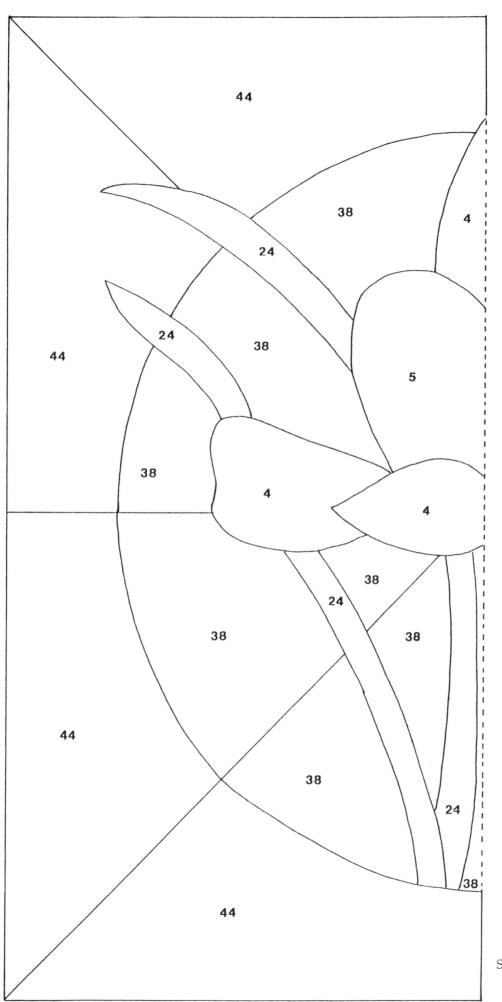

Saffron

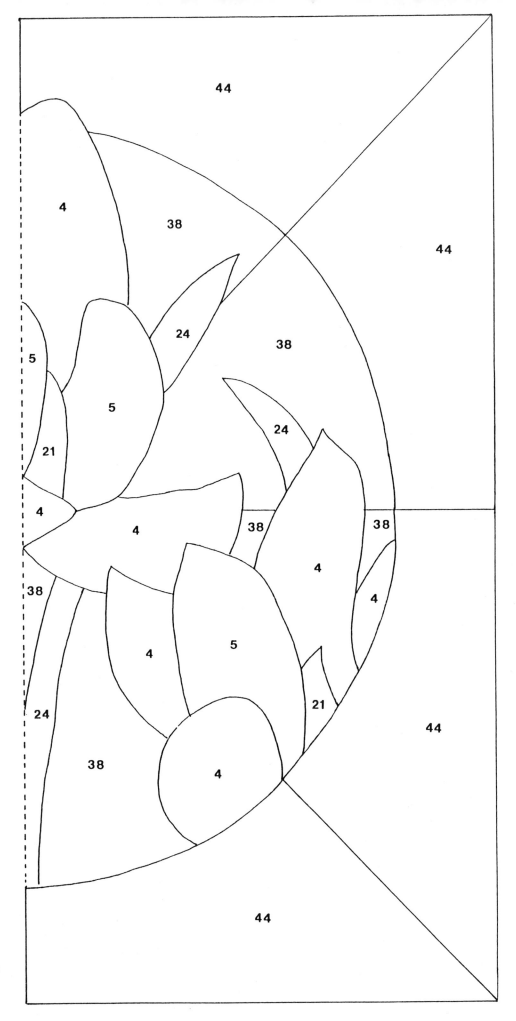

Saffron

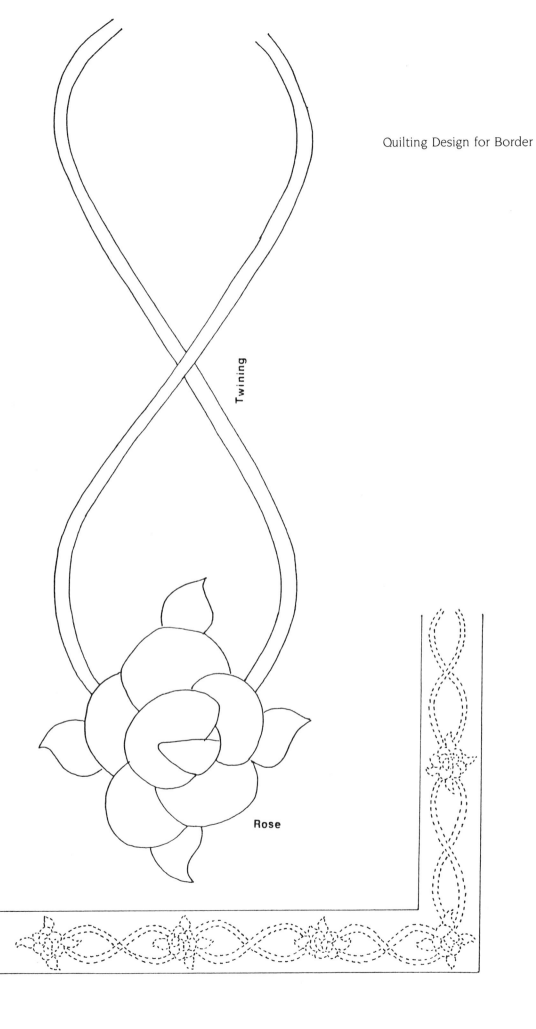

Quilting Design for Border

Twining

Rose

About the Author

Mary E. Dillon is a native Arizonan residing in Tucson. This southwestern influence can be seen in many of her original designs. A lifelong interest and participation in a number of needle arts led her to more extensive work in the quilting field following graduation from the University of Arizona. Fellow quilters will readily understand when she says, "I started quilting as a means of creative outlet, and this rapidly progressed to a complete immersion in the craft." She is involved in all areas of quilting as a designer, lecturer, teacher, and quilt historian. Mary regularly exhibits her art and is the recipient of numerous awards for her piecing, appliqué, and quilting skills. Her study of quilts has given her a strong interest in not only the quilts but also the lives of the quilters and has led her to participate in a number of quilting organizations that strive to promote the art and to preserve quilting history.